W9-BZT-775

All About ADHD

The Complete Practical Guide for Classroom Teachers

Linda J. Pfiffner, Ph.D.

2nd Edition
Revised and Updated

SCHOLASTIC

New York • Toronto • London • Auckland • Sydney
Mexico City • New Delhi • Hong Kong • Buenos Aires

THIS BOOK IS DEDICATED TO:

- *The many teachers across the United States, some of whom shared their innovative ideas for successfully teaching students with ADHD, including:*

  David Agler, Valerie Bonacci, Donna Hall, Hope Hartman, Andrea Hauber, Kathleen Healy, Fran Martin, Lynn McGauly, Mary Olvak, Jay Teeman, Suzanne Vighetti, and Deanne Zyromski

- *Educators, learning support professionals, and families of the San Francisco Unified School District who have helped with our research on developing and evaluating collaborative school-home programs for ADHD*

- *Sarah Glasscock, Joanna Davis-Swing, Virginia Dooley and the rest of the talented staff at Scholastic for their support of this project*

- *Dr. Keith McBurnett for his ongoing support both personally and professionally*

- *and to Kara McBurnett who is a continual source of inspiration and pride*

Acquisition Editor: Joanna Davis-Swing

Editor: Sarah Glasscock

Copy Editor: Chris Borris

Cover Designer: Jaime Lucero

Cover Photography: Copyright © MediaBakery

Interior Designer: Holly Grundon

ISBN: 978-0-545-10920-8

Copyright © 2011 by Linda J. Pfiffner

2 3 4 5 6 7 8 9 10   40   17 16 15 14 13 12 11

CONTENTS

Preface 5

Introduction 6

CHAPTER 1: OVERVIEW OF ADHD 8

What Is ADHD? 8

Subtypes of ADHD 9

ADHD and Girls 15

Executive Functioning Problems 16

Problems That Occur Along With ADHD 16

Outcomes for ADHD During Childhood, Adolescence, and Adulthood 19

Causes of ADHD 22

Underlying Biological Mechanisms and Educational Needs 24

Diagnostic Labels 26

CHAPTER 2: ADHD-FRIENDLY CLASSROOMS 27

Building Positive Relationships With Students 27

Setting Up the Classroom Environment 28

Establishing Routines 32

Delivering Lessons to Maximize Attention 35

Peer-to-Peer Learning 39

Curricula Formats to Enhance Attention 42

Teaching Organizational and Study Skills 48

Teaching Social Skills 52

CHAPTER 3: BEHAVIOR MANAGEMENT BASICS 62

Establishing and Implementing Rules 62

Hand Signals and Visual Prompts 63

Involving Students in Lessons 64

Giving Directions to Increase Compliance 65

Using Your Attention Strategically 68

Integrating Instruction, Rules, and Feedback to Promote
Good Attention and Behavior 72

**CHAPTER 4: INDIVIDUALIZED BEHAVIOR PROGRAMS:
WHEN MORE IS NEEDED** 77

Assessing Behavior 77

Selecting Target Behaviors and Goals 81

Motivating Behavior Change 83

Individual and Classwide Reward Programs 91

Group and Team Reward Programs 98

The Importance of Novelty and Creativity 102

Using a Contract 104

Self-Monitoring and Self-Evaluation 105
Fading Reward Programs 108
The Prudent Use of Negative Consequences 110

CHAPTER 5: THE SCHOOL-HOME CONNECTION: PARENT AND TEACHER PARTNERSHIPS 119
Working Together 119
Homework 120
Long-Term Projects 126
The Daily School-Home Report Card 127
Reverse Daily Report Card 138

CHAPTER 6: DECIDING WHICH PROCEDURES TO USE 140
Teacher Self-Assessment Checklist 141
Putting It All Together: Sample Solutions to
Common Problems of Students With ADHD 144

CHAPTER 7: EVALUATING WHETHER THE PROGRAM IS WORKING 149
How to Avoid Sinking Your Own Ship 149
How to Have an Effective Program 150

CHAPTER 8: ADHD BEYOND THE CLASSROOM 154
How Is ADD/ADHD Identified? 154
The Diagnostic Criteria for ADHD 154
What Should You Do If You Suspect a Student May Have ADHD? 157
What Are the Roles of Professionals in Making a Diagnosis and
Providing Treatment? 158
Educational Identification and Policies Relevant for ADHD 160
What Are the Evidence-Based Treatments for ADHD? 161
Medication Treatments. 162
What Is the Teacher's Role in Medication Treatment? 163
Alternative Treatments 164

CHAPTER 9: THE EFFECTS OF ADHD ON TEACHERS 166
Energizing and Reenergizing for Teachers 167

CHAPTER 10: QUESTIONS AND ANSWERS 168

References and Readings 171
Resources 174
Index 175

PREFACE

Since the first edition of this book, information about ADHD and dissemination of this information to schools has increased dramatically. The U.S. Department of Education's Office of Special Education Programs has released documents about recommended school-based interventions for ADHD, and numerous publications exist on the topic. More and more students with ADHD who attend public schools are being served by special education programs through the Individuals with Disabilities Education Act (IDEA), especially since ADHA was identified as a qualifying condition for special education, or through accommodations in general education classrooms provided by Section 504 of the Rehabilitation Act.

My goal in writing this revision is to provide an update about the latest research on our understanding of ADHD, including etiology, long-term outcomes, and treatments. As in the previous edition, I emphasize best practices for teaching students with ADHD. I have included the latest research outcomes for specific practices and draw upon new real-life examples of interventions teachers have shared with me to pass on to you. I am continually impressed by the innovative practices of the many dedicated and talented teachers I have met across the country. Their enthusiasm for their work is undoubtedly a gift for their students. As in the previous edition, this book intends to bring together the art and science of effective teaching to help you design classrooms that work well not only for students with ADHD but also for all of your students.

INTRODUCTION

An estimated five to seven percent of the school-age population in the United States has attention deficit hyperactivity disorder. Odds are, then, that at least several children in each classroom across the country have ADHD or significant symptoms of the disorder, putting them at risk for adverse educational, and social, outcomes. ADHD is equally prevalent across the world, having been identified in every country in which it has been studied. Children with ADHD in the U.S. and other countries have a similar profile of educational underperformance, social ineptitude, behavioral problems, and adverse health consequences stemming from their primary symptoms of inattention and/or hyperactivity and impulsivity. The average incremental annual cost to educate a student with ADHD is about $4,900 more than for students in regular education, mostly due to special education services and the costs of retention. This comes to over $13 billion in annual costs for students across the country. Adding in other substantial costs associated with ADHD (including funds spent by the juvenile justice, health care, and mental health systems), the incremental annual cost per student can be up to $13,000, making it a major health problem in the U.S. and across the world (Pelham et al., 2007).

Over the past two decades, our understanding of ADHD has sharpened considerably. Research studies have confirmed a hereditary basis in the majority of cases, and several candidate genes hold promise in explaining aspects of the disorder. We have gained an increased understanding of the neuropsychological characteristics of ADHD—especially related to deficits in executive functions—and neuroimaging techniques have linked these characteristics to brain regions and networks. New research is focused on non-hereditary risks, including environmental toxins and pre- and postnatal risk factors. Longitudinal studies consistently show that the disorder is not specific to childhood—without help, a person who has ADHD can experience years of frustration and misunderstanding.

Considerable effort has been made to develop more effective treatments. New longer-acting medications have been developed for the disorder, with positive effects on symptom reduction. A large multisite treatment study of ADHD (MTA Study) confirmed the beneficial short-term effects of medication on symptom reduction (MTA Cooperative Group, 1999).

The effectiveness of behavioral treatments for ADHD, and for school-based interventions in particular, has been confirmed in the MTA study as well as in many other research studies (Wolraich & DuPaul, 2010; Fabiano et al., 2009). The combination of medication and behavioral interventions appears to be the most potent treatment approach. However, recent research shows that sufficiently intense behavioral interventions can reduce medication dosages and sometimes the need for medication altogether (Fabiano, 2007).

Perhaps most important for educators to know is that it is increasingly recognized that changing ADHD behavior in the classroom requires that behavioral treatments be administered in the classroom. In other words, interventions need to be applied where and when the child is having difficulty. Individual therapy sessions in or outside of school do not have much positive impact on ADHD issues in the classroom—the beneficial effects of such therapy rarely generalize. What this means is that your role as teacher is crucial for these students. The extent to which you can engage and motivate them can make all of the difference.

This book is intended to help you do this. We know that classrooms and ADHD left unchecked do not mix well. The need to focus, pay attention, and follow directions goes against the very nature of ADHD children. Many classrooms, such as those with a large teacher-student ratio, provide students with less attention than they need. A tenet of this book is that the problems ADHD children have in school are not due only to a disorder in the child or a problem in the structure of schools. Instead, these problems are aggravated by a mismatch between the classroom and students with ADHD. The key to helping these students is to improve the fit through strategic application of accommodations. Recognizing that many, if not most, students with ADHD are being served in general education classrooms, this requires balancing the individual needs of the few students with ADHD in such classes with the needs of the larger classroom. This means helping all learners in the class, while providing the critical structure needed by the ADHD student.

As you go through this book, it is important to develop an understanding of the general principles underlying successful behavior management of ADHD. You will find examples of effective strategies throughout this book. However, knowing the principles will allow you to develop your own innovative twists to fit your classroom and teaching style. Teachers report that many of the strategies are effective teaching tools for all students. They also say that in some cases the strategies are actually easier to apply when they are used for everyone. We urge you to consider using these strategies to benefit all your students.

A TENET OF THIS BOOK IS THAT THE PROBLEMS ADHD CHILDREN HAVE IN SCHOOL ARE NOT DUE ONLY TO A DISORDER IN THE CHILD OR A PROBLEM IN THE STRUCTURE OF SCHOOLS.

■ ■ ■

CHAPTER 1

OVERVIEW OF ADHD

WHAT IS ADHD?

ADHD, or attention deficit hyperactivity disorder, is a neurodevelop-mental disorder that affects a diverse group of children who have significant problems with inattention, distractibility, and, in many cases, impulsivity and overactivity. These problems cause serious academic and social impairments. The American Psychiatric Association, the American Psychological Association, and the United States Department of Education all recognize ADHD as a serious problem affecting thousands of children every year. Students with ADHD have trouble staying focused, listening, and completing work. Many create disruption in class by calling out, walking around the room during seatwork time, and socializing at inappropriate moments. While all children are inattentive, impulsive, or overactive at times, for ADHD children, these problems are much more extreme and enduring—so much so that they interfere with their ability to function at home and at school, and to develop friendships. In other words, these are not children who occasionally have trouble concentrating and completing their work. These are children with chronic and impairing problems. These problems begin early in life but are often not recognized until a child starts school. Many problems can look like ADHD but actually are another disorder. Being anxious or depressed can cause inattention; so can failing to understand the material being taught. Some medications can also cause inattention and impulsivity. Distinguishing ADHD from such problems and from the normal range of children's attentiveness and activity requires a comprehensive evaluation by a trained professional (see Chapter 8). ADHD is not due to laziness, academic slowness, or poor parenting. ADHD is not something learned, and it is not something kids choose to have. No one is to blame for ADHD. It is considered to be a neurobiological or neurobehavioral condition that usually requires special intervention. Although there is not a cure for the disorder, you, as an educator, can use strategies like the ones in this book to help these children be successful.

SUBTYPES OF ADHD

Over the past century, many diagnostic labels have been applied to children with ADHD. The fourth edition of the *Diagnostic and Statistical Manual of Mental Disorders* (*DSM-IV*, 1994), published by the American Psychiatric Association, provides the official criteria for a diagnosis of ADHD. This manual is used to identify the full range of child and adult mental health disorders by medical and mental health professionals across the country and is revised periodically to reflect changes in our understanding of mental health disorders based on research studies. In the *DSM-IV*, characteristics or symptoms of ADHD are divided into two categories: 1) inattention, and 2) hyperactivity-impulsivity. There are three subtypes of ADHD based on whether there are problems in one or both of these categories:

- ➲ ADHD-combined type, in which both inattention and hyperactivity/impulsivity are present

- ➲ ADHD-predominantly inattentive type, in which only inattention is present

- ➲ ADHD-predominantly hyperactive/impulsive type, in which only hyperactivity and impulsivity are present

ADHD-COMBINED SUBTYPE

ADHD-combined type is the "classic" variety of ADHD and is the most common type referred to clinics for evaluations and treatment. Although these kids can be quite different from one another, they share the same core characteristics. Most don't pay close attention to group lessons or individual tasks (particularly repetitive, uninteresting ones). When they do attend, they often pick the wrong information to focus on. Many have a hard time starting and stopping tasks and shifting from one thing to another. They interrupt and call out in class, they can't seem to focus or stay quiet, and they are easily frustrated and bored. They often have difficulty regulating their emotions and may be prone to "outbursts." They are often "risk takers" and disregard rules that don't meet their immediate needs. Assignments are often completed in haste. They can be fun-loving and engaging but don't know when to quit. Many of these children are at risk for aggressive behavior and conduct problems. Repeated failure with peers and poor grades often chip away at the self-esteem of many of these children as they get older. Here are some of the common problems experienced by the ADHD-combined subtype.

COMMON PROBLEMS IN CLASS

- ⮑ overly active
- ⮑ doesn't sit still
- ⮑ falls out of seat
- ⮑ fiddles with things
- ⮑ too talkative
- ⮑ calls out without raising hand
- ⮑ impatient
- ⮑ fails to start work
- ⮑ work completed is sloppy
- ⮑ class clown
- ⮑ wants peer attention
- ⮑ doesn't accept consequences
- ⮑ easily frustrated
- ⮑ doesn't adhere to rules
- ⮑ noisy and disruptive
- ⮑ wants immediate gratification
- ⮑ difficulty persisting with uninteresting activities
- ⮑ messy and disorganized

COMMON PROBLEMS WITH PEERS

- ⮑ physically intrusive
- ⮑ touchy
- ⮑ butts into activities
- ⮑ easily frustrated
- ⮑ bossy
- ⮑ insists on own way
- ⮑ misses social cues

EVAN, AGE 8

DIAGNOSIS: ADHD-combined type

Evan's mother noticed her son seemed more rambunctious than her other children when he was a toddler. Relatives often commented that he was "all boy." In preschool, the teacher reported Evan had difficulty staying with the group during circle time, often wandering around and getting into things. He often bothered the other children and resisted nap time. His mother hoped he would settle down when he started elementary school. In kindergarten, Evan did seem to do a bit better. His teacher took him under her wing, giving him accommodations when it was needed. To keep close tabs on Evan's behavior and to prevent off-task activities, she kept him physically close to her (e.g., sitting next to her during circle time and placing his desk next to hers during seatwork time). She also made sure he understood each task, and she used rewards when he was doing what he was supposed to be doing. In first grade, Evan became increasingly disruptive and silly. His teacher recommended that he be evaluated for ADHD, but his mother decided to hold off, reasoning that some of his behavior was due to the lack of structure in the class and the fact that there were a number of active boys. Problems continued into second grade. In addition to behavioral issues, Evan was beginning to be rejected by his classmates. Now in third grade, problems have worsened. Evan is disruptive, rarely stays focused on his work, and increasingly misses out on many learning opportunities. His teacher notices that his behavior is bothering his classmates—he is noisy, messy, and his body and belongings overflow to his classmates' desks. Evan often fails to play fairly on the playground and has a reputation for not being a good sport. He has been asked not to return to an after-school class due to his lack of self-control. His mother reports homework is a battle, as is getting him out of the house on time in the morning. Evan is rarely asked over to play with children his age. His mother is concerned that he doesn't want to go to school.

- doesn't inhibit inappropriate comments
- can't see others' viewpoints
- doesn't ignore provocation
- wants to switch activities too often
- rejected by peers

COMMON PROBLEMS AT HOME

- doesn't listen
- rushes through or fails to complete homework
- interrupts conversations
- doesn't put things away
- quick to lose temper when needs not met
- forgets chores
- dawdles in the morning
- hates to wait
- acts before thinking
- reckless
- lacks independence in self-care

ADHD-PREDOMINANTLY INATTENTIVE SUBTYPE

Many children have ADHD-predominantly inattentive subtype, formally known as ADD without hyperactivity. This is the most common type of ADHD in school settings. These kids are not those usually thought to have ADHD because they are not overly active. In fact, they may be underactive or lethargic. These are kids who are extremely inattentive. They can't stay focused for long on a task and seem to spend inordinate amounts of time daydreaming. They are often quiet and go unnoticed in a large classroom. They may seem to be "just lazy" or not trying, but actually, they have great difficulty concentrating and controlling their streams of thought. They are very disorganized and forgetful, and they need close supervision to get through a task. They seem to be confused about things like which page they should be on in the middle of a group lesson or what their assignment is for homework. It takes a lot of effort for them to shift their attention from one thing to another, just as it is hard for them to focus on any one thing for long. Their work is often incomplete. They are often very aware of their problems and insecure about their abilities. Self-esteem is often low.

Here are some common problems experienced by the ADHD-predominantly inattentive type.

COMMON PROBLEMS IN CLASS

- daydreams
- doesn't complete work
- forgetful
- fails to attend to details
- seems tired
- "in a fog"
- disorganized
- loses things
- messy desk
- needs close supervision to stay on task
- may have learning problems
- great difficulty attending to tasks
- easily distracted by internal and external stimuli

COMMON PROBLEMS WITH PEERS

- withdrawn
- quiet
- ignored by peers
- socially immature
- inattentive during conversations

COMMON PROBLEMS AT HOME

- homework not completed
- chores forgotten
- needs constant reminders
- messy and disorganized
- always losing things
- spacey
- doesn't seem to listen

CASE EXAMPLE

MARIA, AGE 11
DIAGNOSIS:
ADHD-predominantly inattentive

Maria was a very well-behaved and mellow child. Her preschool teacher described her as being a sweet girl, although somewhat shy. In kindergarten, she always followed class rules but continued to be quiet—she did not participate in class discussions very often and did not make friends easily. In first through third grades, teachers often commented that Maria would drift off during class and miss class instruction, causing her to miss assignments. Her desk area was often disorganized and messy. She did not have many friends and was not an active participant in class. By fifth grade, Maria's teacher became more concerned. Her disorganization was not improving. As the demands for independence were increasing (students were now required to write down assignments rather than being given a weekly list of assignments from the teachers), she had trouble meeting them. She struggled to keep track of assignments and was also very slow in getting her work done—which was more problematic now that the workload was increased. Socially, Maria continued to have few friends, and she seemed young for her age. At home, her parents reported she had great difficulty completing her homework—what was supposed to take 40 minutes ended up taking her three hours. Maria's parents were also concerned about her spaciness and failure to follow through on daily routine activities like getting ready for school and doing her chores.

ADHD-PREDOMINANTLY HYPERACTIVE IMPULSIVE SUBTYPE

These are kids who are overly active and impulsive, but not currently showing signs of too many difficulties with inattention. About half of the kids or more with this subtype are in first grade or younger, predominantly in preschool. Research shows that many of these younger kids start showing signs of inattention as they become old enough to encounter academic seatwork. This means many end up meeting the criteria for ADHD-combined subtype by the time they are in middle elementary school. Although less is known about this subtype than the others, it appears to be associated with disruptive behavior, aggression, and peer problems more so than academic deficiencies.

Note: There is often a point of confusion about the terms ADHD and ADD (attention deficit disorder) as applied to those with attention deficits but not the hyperactivity component. As noted earlier, the current diagnostic term used in research as well as professional and medical communities is ADHD. This is an umbrella term which includes all of the ADHD subtypes (for example, those with or without hyperactivity/impulsivity). In order to be consistent with current practice, and for simplicity, we use the term "ADHD" in this book to include those children with any of the subtypes of ADHD (i.e., with or without the hyperactivity/impulsivity component).

A word about severity: Along with differences in the types of problems they have, kids with ADHD differ in terms of the severity of their problems. For some kids, ADHD can be quite severe and disabling; for others it may be just a mild annoyance. Even the severity can vary from hour to hour and day to day. Problems may be virtually absent in some situations. Perhaps one of the most difficult things about the disorder is its variability. Teachers often comment, "He seems to do well on some days, and is even a model student at times. But then, for no reason, he falls apart." Parents often say, "He can play computer games for hours. Why can't he pay attention to his homework for more than two minutes?" Remember, variability is part of ADHD. The conditions causing and affecting the disorder are not static. Also, don't interpret the behavior as being willful. If these kids could be successful every day, they would be.

ADHD AND GIRLS

ADHD is more common in boys than in girls (three boys to every girl); even so, thousands of girls have the disorder (Hinshaw & Blachman, 2005). Girls with ADHD are different from boys in that they are less often disruptive and physically aggressive and more likely to have the inattentive type of ADHD. Girls may be more likely than boys to exhibit relational aggression (e.g., exclude peers, spread rumors, gossip, tell lies) and they may be at increased risk of eating disorders. They may also be more at risk for negative peer experiences (peer rejection, fewer dyadic friendships) due to the greater salience of their high activity and impulsivity and their often co-occurring language and cognitive problems which may interfere with the emphasis on verbal interchanges in girl friendships. In most other ways,

GIRLS WITH ADHD ARE DIFFERENT FROM BOYS IN THAT THEY ARE LESS OFTEN DISRUPTIVE AND PHYSICALLY AGGRESSIVE AND MORE LIKELY TO HAVE THE INATTENTIVE TYPE OF ADHD.

■ ■ ■

they show the same impairments across domains as their male counterparts and have the same response to treatment. Most girls do not grow out of their problems, and they have a similar negative trajectory across domains of impairment. The risk for girls is that the condition is often undetected, and so untreated, because they often lack the disruptive components and because ADHD is often thought of as a boy's disorder.

EXECUTIVE FUNCTIONING PROBLEMS

Accumulating research suggests that deficits in what's referred to as "executive functioning" are prominent among children with ADHD. Executive functioning includes skills such as planning, prioritizing, organizing, regulating one's own behavior, moods, and motivation, time management, and working memory. To better understand executive functioning, consider an orchestra analogy. The conductor of the orchestra represents the part of the brain in charge of managing and coordinating the remaining brain areas, which for this analogy are the musical instruments. When the conductor is asleep, all the different instruments are free to play in any way they want. Each musician might be very talented, but there is no coordination and the quality of the music suffers. When the conductor is awake and managing the orchestra, he or she does so by alternately directing some instruments to be quiet and others to play. The conductor manages all of the individual instruments in an organized way to create beautiful music. Students with ADHD have many talents and skills, but the conductor is often asleep!

Difficulties with executive functioning have many ramifications for the classroom and for the development of independent skills. Students with executive functioning problems will have trouble planning in advance how to allot time to various projects or anticipate issues that may arise. They may not start projects until the deadline is imminent or even past. They may feel overwhelmed with multitasking and prioritizing. They may react impulsively without considering consequences.

PROBLEMS THAT OCCUR ALONG WITH ADHD

Many children with ADHD have other problems, such as oppositional behavior, anxiety, depression, or learning disabilities. If these problems are severe enough, additional diagnoses may be made. These problems often require more intensive interventions.

ADHD AND OPPOSITIONAL/ CONDUCT PROBLEMS

More than half of the children who have ADHD are also very stubborn, defiant, and aggressive (Barkley, 2006). When sufficiently chronic and severe, these problems make up a separate disorder called oppositional defiant disorder (ODD). As suggested by the name, these are children who are overtly disobedient toward authority figures such as teachers and parents. They refuse to follow rules, and they use temper tantrums and arguments to try to get their way. They may seem to have a "chip on their shoulder" and appear chronically angry and resentful. Little things may set them off and they may constantly blame other people for their mishaps. The combination of ADHD and ODD is very challenging. Even more disabling is conduct disorder, which affects as many as 30 percent of children with ADHD (Barkley, 2006). Children with conduct disorder have a pattern of breaking society's rules. They may lie, steal, run away, set fires, destroy property, or start physical fights. Often these symptoms don't emerge until the middle or high school years.

MICHAEL, AGE 7

DIAGNOSIS: ADHD with oppositional defiant disorder

CASE EXAMPLE

For Michael, the terrible twos never ended. His mother reports that, over the years, it has been very difficult to manage his behavior at home, especially his arguing and tantrumming when something does not go his way. At preschool, his teacher called Michael's mother after the first week to say he was disobedient and too physical with his classmates. When Michael started kindergarten, he quickly developed a reputation for having behavioral problems, which continued to his present second-grade classroom. He is impulsive, quick to react, and defiant to teachers and staff. Michael has trouble staying in his seat and often calls out. Although he can do the assigned work, he often fails to complete it. On the playground, Michael is aggressive and bossy, and although he is often with other children, he does not have any real friends. His mother notices frequent conflict between him and his brother. She seldom asks Michael to do anything, because compliance is such a battle.

ADHD AND EMOTIONAL PROBLEMS

Emotional disorders such as anxiety or depression also often accompany ADHD, with estimates of its occurrence ranging from 13 to over 50 percent. Emotional disorders may arise independently or may be an outgrowth of ADHD, so it becomes important to clarify if a child's inattention is due to ADHD or an emotional disorder (or both) since anxiety and depression can also cause inattention. Kids with both ADHD and an anxiety disorder may be more disabled by the anxiety they feel than by the symptoms of ADHD. They are often overly and, at times, obsessively worried about things in their lives. Some kids may worry about being apart from their parents. Others may worry about meeting new people or trying new things. Some may worry about what their classmates think of them or what their teachers think of them. They may also worry about their ADHD symptoms: forgetfulness, disorganization, and so on. For some kids, anxiety may be expressed through acting out.

Not surprisingly, many ADHD kids are also depressed. The repeated failures and frustrations they experience can take a toll. Even if the majority are not "clinically depressed," many are demoralized, feel poorly about themselves, and feel hopeless about changing their circumstances. Frequently, kids who are depressed appear to be chronically irritable or angry rather than sad. They may have lost interest in things they once enjoyed, and they may avoid being around other kids. Their self-esteem can be quite fragile. They often misinterpret others' actions and seem to have a veil of pessimism that darkens their world.

Although the many difficulties faced by children with ADHD can adversely impact their self-esteem, this does not always seem to be the case. Research shows that some children with ADHD have overly positive views of themselves and their competencies (Kaiser & Hoza, 2008). They may have limited awareness about their own skills and abilities due to their executive functioning problems and lack of self-regulation and insight. They may come across as boastful or overly confident as a façade for feelings of insecurity. Alternatively, they may lack an understanding of what constitutes competence and thus be unable to accurately evaluate their own behavior. Their overly positive self-views may interfere with their motivations to modify their inappropriate behavior.

ADHD AND LEARNING OR LANGUAGE PROBLEMS

As many as one out of three children identified with ADHD also have a learning disorder (DuPaul & Stoner, 2003). A learning disorder may be related to deficits in areas such as language processing, auditory processing, visual-spatial processing, or visual-perceptual processing. A learning disorder is typically defined by impaired performance on specific standardized tests of language abilities, nonverbal abilities, and/or achievement. If significant discrepancies are found between performance on such tests and overall intellectual ability, a learning disorder may be identified in one or more skill areas such as reading, mathematics, spelling, or language. These deficits are not simply the result of inattention; they constitute a separate processing problem. Symptoms of ADHD can exacerbate learning problems, and vice versa. For those students who have ADHD but not a learning disorder, inattention to task, distractibility, and impulsivity can still interfere with their ability to complete work satisfactorily, although they score well on standardized tests, especially if they are administered in a one-on-one setting, relatively free from distraction. Because of the frequent co-occurrence of learning disorders, it is important to specifically assess for learning and language problems when academic performance is low.

MOTOR CONTROL PROBLEMS

Problems of motor control are also often found among children with ADHD, although they are not part of the diagnosis. Motor problems can include clumsiness, which might be due to primary motor problems (muscle coordination, balance) or are secondary to impulsivity and overactivity. Commonly, students with ADHD have handwriting difficulties caused by fine motor control deficits. These difficulties may be helped by strength training or by the use of adaptive writing tools. However, training the student in keyboarding skills is usually more beneficial since less fine motor control is required.

OUTCOMES FOR ADHD DURING CHILDHOOD, ADOLESCENCE, AND ADULTHOOD

ADHD begins early in life and generally follows a chronic course. A number of longitudinal studies following children with ADHD into adulthood show that up to 80 percent continue to meet criteria for the disorder during adolescence. While fewer do so in adulthood, those who had ADHD as children often continue to be plagued by ongoing adverse impacts in their daily lives as adults (Barkley, 2006). The kinds of problems associated with ADHD usually change as one gets older. Some typical patterns are described below.

Preschool: The first signs of ADHD often include high activity, low tolerance for frustration, and the need for constant supervision in toddlerhood and preschool. Features of inattention and overactivity are common in preschoolers and often outgrown. Nevertheless, 70 percent of preschoolers with a diagnosis of ADHD continue to meet criteria for the disorder during elementary school. In addition, they often have the following outcomes:

- Frequent accidents due to impulsivity

- Problematic peer relations due to grabbing, pushing, and not following rules

- Management problems in preschool due to trouble sitting through circle time, following rules, and staying with activities

- Lack of basic academic readiness skills needed for kindergarten

- School failures (including expulsions) before kindergarten

Elementary school: This is often the time when ADHD is first identified. Most research on ADHD has been conducted with this age group. The following outcomes are common:

- Management problems in class due to difficulty following teacher directions and classroom rules

- 90 percent or more show poor school performance— incomplete/inaccurate assignments and/or low academic achievement

- Low report card grades, especially in work habits

- Peer relationship problems (more than half), including rejection and/or neglect

- Two-to-three year lag in social maturity

- High level of parent-child conflict and stress

- Oppositional or conduct problems (half or more) along with ADHD

Middle school and high school: Struggles with self-control continue and organizational problems are exacerbated by having multiple classes and teachers. Some symptoms may become less extreme (especially the overactivity) but are still apparent. Common outcomes for children identified with ADHD during adolescence include the following:

- 80 percent continue to meet criteria for ADHD
- 25–45 percent retained in a grade
- 40–60 percent suspended
- 10–18 percent expelled
- 30–40 percent drop out
- 25–55 percent have oppositional or conduct problems
- Earlier experimentation with and greater risk for substance abuse
- More at-fault car accidents and traffic tickets
- More teen pregnancies and STDs
- Greater hospitalizations and higher medical costs
- Poor outcomes exacerbated by presence of conduct problems

Adulthood: The good news is that a third to one half of adults who had ADHD as children do quite well in the adult world. They may choose occupations such as sales, entertainment, and business ownership, where their "symptoms" may actually be assets. However, others do not fare as well, as seen in the following statistics from long-term outcome studies comparing those with ADHD versus those without:

- Greater unemployment
- More likely to be fired
- Lower work performance ratings
- Lower job status rating and socioeconomic status
- More motor vehicle accidents (two to three times the risk) and speeding citations
- More expensive auto accidents and suspensions or revocations of license
- More arrests and antisocial behavior
- Higher rates of substance abuse and depression
- Higher rates of divorce

Those with the least favorable outcomes seem to have had severe and chronic conduct problems in addition to ADHD as children.

While diversity is the norm for ADHD and its course over the years, one thing is clear: It is not outgrown. The key is to match environments to individual needs and strategically plan for adult outcomes. The answer is not to "wait and see."

CAUSES OF ADHD

Within the last two decades, numerous studies have confirmed that ADHD is a neurobiological condition. Evidence for this comes from studies of brain function, genetic and non-genetic physical environmental factors, the results of which are described below. Leading theories and research studies point to genetic and non-genetic physical causes, but not social causes, for ADHD.

Differences in brain function: Brain imaging techniques allow researchers to compare the size and activation patterns of the brain. Studies using these techniques show that the areas of the brain that regulate impulses, attention, and behavior are smaller and less active in children with ADHD compared to those without ADHD (Barkley, 2006). These studies also provide evidence for reduced sensitivity to reinforcement in ADHD. Additionally, slower brain waves are observed on the EEGs of individuals with ADHD, signifying lower arousal. Abnormalities have been associated with the prefrontal cortex, basal ganglia, cerebellum, and corpus callosum. However, the underlying abnormality does not appear to be limited to a discrete brain area; instead, it appears that the circuitry connecting the frontal area with these areas of the brain is what's impacted in ADHD.

Genetics: The most frequent cause of ADHD is heredity; that is, children inherit the condition from one or both parents. Up to a third or more of the parents and siblings of children with ADHD have the disorder themselves. More than half of children of parents with ADHD have it themselves. Studies with identical and fraternal twins give us information about the relative influence of genes and environment on ADHD. Results of these studies show that about 80 percent of the variance in ADHD traits is due to genetics. In fact, ADHD appears to be almost as heritable as height. It is not yet known which genes are involved in the transmission of ADHD. Studies of molecular genetics in which the DNA of children is evaluated identify several genes that may contribute to ADHD. These genes are predominantly associated with brain systems involving the neurotransmitter dopamine, although other transmitters and systems have also been linked to ADHD. It is likely that ADHD involves multiple genes and systems. Even though a genetic basis for the disorder is likely in most cases, it is important to point out that these genetic effects may be moderated by environmental factors.

Environmental factors: ADHD can be the result of low birth weight or other complications during pregnancy or birth (e.g., toxemia). Prenatal exposure to nicotine, as well as other drugs and alcohol, can lead to ADHD and ADHD-like behaviors. Exposure to environmental toxins after birth may also lead to ADHD. The most notable and well-studied among these is lead, which has been shown to affect learning, attention, and behavior. While the adverse effects of high lead exposures are clear, recent evidence also suggests some risk for low-level lead exposure, which is currently being investigated (Nigg, 2006). Exposure to other toxins such as mercury, manganese, and PCBs has also been associated with cognitive and attentional problems, although evidence of association with ADHD is less clear. While dietary explanations for ADHD are unlikely (with no evidence supporting sugar intake or caffeine as causal factors), fatty acid deficiencies and exposure to pesticides may contribute. However, it should be noted that these dietary factors and environmental toxin risks are most likely to be related to ADHD through complicated gene-environment interactions. Researchers are just beginning to study how factors such as environmental toxins might interact with genetic vulnerability to increase the risk for ADHD. Television viewing during early childhood has also been studied in relation to ADHD. There appears to be a weak association between ADHD and TV viewing, but a causal relationship between them has not been found. Instead, children with ADHD may be more inclined to watch TV than to engage in other activities requiring sustained attention. On the other hand, a significant causal connection between violent TV programming and increased aggressive behavior in children at risk for behavior problems has been found. Given the risk of aggression among children with ADHD, these findings indicate the need to minimize exposure to such programming.

Social environmental factors do NOT cause ADHD: This means that parenting styles and teaching strategies do not play causal roles. However, they can affect the severity of problems. We know that certain teaching styles are more helpful for students with ADHD than are others. Children with ADHD do well in one-on-one situations where there is lots of supervision and redirection to task. They also do well during novel, stimulating activities and in highly reinforcing situations. Take for example their attraction to computer games, which, much to their parents' dismay, they can play for hours on end. Computer games meet the basic requirements necessary to capture the interest of children with ADHD: they are very stimulating and offer frequent, immediate positive reinforcement.

WE KNOW THAT CERTAIN TEACHING STYLES ARE MORE HELPFUL FOR STUDENTS WITH ADHD THAN ARE OTHERS.

■ ■ ■

The moderating effect of the environment on ADHD is good news. It means that you as a teacher can make a positive difference.

UNDERLYING BIOLOGICAL MECHANISMS AND EDUCATIONAL NEEDS

These theories center around problems with executive functions/cognitive control, arousal, motivation, and motor control and timing (Nigg, 2006). Researchers using brain-imaging and psycho-physiological techniques have documented abnormalities associated with ADHD that support the following explanations.

Difficulties in the brain systems underlying executive functioning/cognitive control are impacted in ADHD. Several key areas of deficit within these systems include working memory, inhibition, and self-regulation. These deficits help explain why children with ADHD have trouble staying organized, regulating their attention and behavior according to rules and plans, inhibiting impulses, and blocking out distractions. Deficits in working memory may specifically underlie the all-too-common academic problem encountered among children with ADHD: remembering to write down the homework assignment each day in the face of multiple distractions and interruptions going on in the classroom.

Difficulties in the brain systems related to arousal are increasingly associated with apparent attention problems. Children with ADHD exhibit low cortical arousal, which is associated with low alertness. This lack of alertness is similar to what it is like when we are tired, but in the case of ADHD, more sleep does not fix the problem. Instead, this chronic underarousal makes it difficult for children to control and regulate their attention, particularly during activities they find boring or uninteresting. These deficits may explain why ADHD children often behave as if they are trying to increase their arousal level by seeking stimulation and excitement, or why they are able to pay close attention when they are highly stimulated during fast-paced videogames or television programs.

In addition, accumulating evidence indicates that there are important differences in the brain systems that process information about rewards and punishment. Numerous studies clearly demonstrate that children with ADHD perform more poorly than those without ADHD when external contingencies (rewards and punishments) are not used. Research shows that

ADHD is linked to an elevated reward threshold—meaning that children with the disorder need more consistent rewards than typical children to achieve the same goal. This is particularly true when it comes to difficult or low-interest tasks. Students with ADHD also seek immediate reinforcement (even more so than other children) and exhibit what's been termed "delay aversion." That is, they show much greater frustration and many more performance problems when rewards are delayed or not forthcoming (the natural state of affairs in most real-life situations!). These findings explain why the kinds of rewards and punishments that work for most students in the classroom are not sufficient to keep the ADHD student on track.

Faulty interactions between deficient arousal, executive, and/or motivational systems can be particularly impairing. For example, good planning involves anticipating events and considering response options and their associated outcomes. Children with ADHD are often so driven by the need for an immediate reward that they lack the ability to apply their relatively weak attention and executive processes to problem solve. As an example, when faced with the task of completing a packet of worksheets, children with ADHD are less apt to muster their weak attentional resources to orient to the work, to consider the consequences of not completing the work, and to problem solve how to break down the task. Conversely, they are more apt to impulsively engage in an activity they find more entertaining at that moment (e.g., talking to their table mates, playing with something in their desk, wandering around the classroom).

Considering ADHD from these perspectives helps us identify educational strategies that are likely to be successful. The best strategies are those that change the classroom to promote greater cognitive control, stimulation, motivation, and regulation of behavior. The most effective classrooms include the following:

1. **structure:** clear rules, routines, directions, and expectations

2. **salience:** use of visual cues, prompting, repetition of instructions

3. **consistency:** clear limits, use of prudent corrective feedback

4. **motivation:** frequent positive feedback and consequences

5. **interesting lessons:** creative and unique units that engage the child and capture his or her imagination and curiosity

You will find each of these five themes in interventions throughout this book. As you proceed, remember that the intensity of the intervention will vary with the severity and specific problems of the child. For those with the most severe problems, a small class with a small teacher-to-student ratio is optimal. For the mild to moderate cases, a number of accommodations to the regular classroom may be all that is necessary. To foster self-esteem and growth, build on a student's areas of strength rather than focusing only on remediation.

Teachers who work effectively with ADHD children agree that it takes a lot of work, especially at the beginning. Expect to spend more time, energy, and effort in working with an ADHD student. You will need to be more involved with the student and the student's family. It may seem to be an uphill battle at times. But as one teacher noted, "The mountain was hard to climb, but reaching the top deepened my relationship with the student and my sense of being a teacher in a way that wouldn't have happened if the mountain had not been there."

DIAGNOSTIC LABELS

Diagnostic labels like ADHD have many advantages. First of all, knowing a child is ADHD suggests the need for certain treatments and also may qualify the child for services that he or she may not otherwise receive. The ADHD label can also relieve children and parents alike. Knowing that they have ADHD helps kids realize that they are not stupid, even though they may have trouble paying attention or completing all of their work at school. Nevertheless, labels have many problems and limitations. Some kids who find out they have ADHD begin to think that they can't do well in school, or they start using it as an excuse. Self-esteem can suffer because they think something is wrong with them. Some teachers and parents give up on a child who has ADHD. Some parents feel guilty because they think it is their fault. They may not realize that the problems students with ADHD have can be addressed by making small changes in the classroom or at home. Finally, the label ADHD does not describe the whole child. Kids with ADHD are very different from one another. Knowing a child has the disorder does not tell you about his or her unique strengths and talents, it does not tell you about his or her interests or dreams. Likewise, it does not tell you about the specific kinds of things that a child needs help in to be successful. It is usually best to focus less on labels and more on specific goals and behaviors. We may not be able to get rid of ADHD, but we can help students change certain behaviors and meet specific goals.

CHAPTER 2

ADHD-FRIENDLY CLASSROOMS

BUILDING POSITIVE RELATIONSHIPS WITH STUDENTS

The importance of valuing the individuality of each student may be especially crucial in the case of ADHD. Many of these students have been the recipient of repeated criticisms and negativity over the years, and have experienced little success in the classroom or with their peers. Research clearly shows that more negative teacher-student interactions are associated with less student engagement and success, and that more positive interactions are associated with greater academic performance, social skills, and emotion regulation. Teachers who are able to connect with the personal interests of the student and communicate a genuine appreciation for the student's positive attributes and interests are likely to instill greater motivation and cooperation. Long-term studies suggest that successful adults with ADHD recall that it was often a single teacher who served as a turning point in their lives. This teacher was someone who believed in them and did not give up.

It is also necessary that classroom management practices are in place to strategically promote good attention and behavior necessary for academic and social success. You can do this by setting up your classroom environment and using instructional strategies and curricula formats in a way that facilitates a high state of learning readiness (discussed below). These proactive programs are key. They are often the simplest to implement, are useful for the entire class, and can prevent more serious problems from developing. Equally important is to keep your students on track through your strategic delivery of clear directions, praise, and corrective feedback in each lecture, group discussion, cooperative learning group, and independent work period. Guidelines for these are presented in Chapter 3. More intensive, tailored behavior management programs are often needed in severe cases and are presented in Chapter 4.

SETTING UP THE CLASSROOM ENVIRONMENT

The physical arrangement of your classroom can either facilitate or impede learning opportunities and behavior management. For students with ADHD, keep in mind the need for structure, clear physical boundaries, teacher proximity, visual stimulation, and minimal outside distractions. Teachers who have orderly systems to list assignments, keep track of materials, and organize work spaces (including the teacher's desk) make learning easier and serve as good models for students. Take a seat at one of your student's desks and ask yourself if this classroom is a stimulating place to be. Also consider that inattention is exacerbated when students can't read the whiteboard due to poor lighting or glare or small lettering. Take a seat at each desk and make sure everyone can view lectures and visual aids clearly. Consider the following recommendations:

Use preferential seating. Seat the student away from distractions and close to the teaching action. In most classrooms this means seating the child:

- ➲ close to the front of the class (or by your desk or whiteboard) so you can continually monitor his or her work

- ➲ by peers who are good workers (not next to the child's best friend)

- ➲ away from the window, pencil sharpener, hanging mobile, door, or anything else that is interesting or distracting; if you teach in a less structured or eclectic classroom, seat the student away from the open, shared space

- ➲ facing you and the whiteboard so the student won't have to reposition himself to see ongoing instruction

Some teachers place their "problem" students at the back of the class or in an isolated spot to limit their disruptive effect on other students. Sometimes this works well for kids who need more space. However, placement out of direct vision of the teacher usually creates problems. If you do have students with ADHD sitting away from your usual teaching spot, walk by their desks regularly to make sure they understand the assignment and are working on it.

Organize seating to provide clear boundaries for students' work areas. Individual desks with attached chairs are usually better than tables for doing independent seatwork. Students with ADHD often have difficulty with physical boundaries and tend to annoy their peers by "getting in their space." Tables with many students do not usually provide clear enough divisions between students and tend to promote excess socializing. To facilitate group discussion and cooperative learning projects, individual desks or small tables can be grouped together in small clusters. Keep in mind that students with ADHD may require more distance between their desks than will other students. Seating students with attentional concerns at the end of a row allows for quick access to those who might need redirection, and it also gives active students room to stand while completing their work, if need be.

For the kindergarten student, seating arrangements during rug time should also be carefully planned. The area in which the student sits on the floor should have clear boundaries. A carpet square often works well. Another strategy would be to designate the perimeter of personal space during seatwork using a piece of tape. The tape would serve as a visual cue for the student's personal space—inside the taped area would be the student's area; outside would be off limits during seatwork.

You might also have the student sit next to you for close monitoring. Students who are distracted or are having trouble concentrating on their work could also be separated from distractions by sitting at a special quiet table—presented as a privilege rather than a punishment. One teacher decorated an antique desk for this purpose. **A note about standing:** Many students with ADHD simply cannot sit in one place for the time necessary to complete their work. Allow them to stand while working as long as they are not disruptive.

Have a well-organized classroom. While most children and teachers benefit from an organized classroom, the benefits for children with ADHD are even greater. These students typically have difficulty organizing their own space, are easily distracted, and seem to take advantage of (often unintentionally) any opportunity to go off task. When given a direction to do something that involves leaving their seat (e.g., get materials, go to work at a center), they often take the most circuitous route, and end up losing track of what they were told to do. If they do get to the right place, they are easily led astray by something more interesting than the task at hand (e.g., colorful art supplies or pictures, a book, a bug on the wall), especially if they can't find what they need right away. To prevent these kinds of problems, keep

WHILE MOST CHILDREN AND TEACHERS BENEFIT FROM AN ORGANIZED CLASSROOM, THE BENEFITS FOR CHILDREN WITH ADHD ARE EVEN GREATER.

■ ■ ■

centers uncluttered and in order. Have all the materials you need prepared each day before class. Keep supplies and materials stocked and in well-marked areas to which you and your students can have easy access. Using words and picture cues on bookcases and shelves can help students match materials with their storage locations. Color-coding books and materials can also be helpful. Also, use sturdy containers to prevent spills. Minor accidents (dropping a container of pencils or a stack of paper) can become a disruptive event for the whole class when a student with ADHD is involved. Also, keep in mind that students with ADHD often lose pencils, papers, and books. Have plenty of replacements available.

Promote clutter-free desks. To control the clutter at student desks, limit the materials they are allowed to have in or at their desks (e.g., two pencils, two erasers, daily agenda/planner, workbooks, subject folders). The rest goes in their cubby. Remove distracting, unnecessary items from desks (toys, rubber bands, trash, food, and so on). Create a logical order for placement of items. Monitor desks regularly and assist with reorganization as needed.

Give all students a chance to post their best work and feel proud. It was once thought that kids with ADHD needed to be seated in white cubicles, free from any visual input. We now recognize the importance of novelty and creativity in the learning process. Bulletin boards can be a wonderful asset to learning. Enhance them through the use of color, relevant topics and examples, and student contributions. Feel free to create interesting visual displays. Have kids participate in creating the displays for each unit and post their completed work. Post the work of all students, not just the conventionally exceptional work of some students.

Post prominent and interesting visual aids. Put up charts, banners, and diagrams on walls to stimulate students' curiosity about the current subject matter. Also, post inspirational messages and reminders to stay on task. Fran Martin, a teacher at Paddock Lane Elementary in Beatrice, Nebraska, uses big charts posted around her room with inspirational messages for students ("10 Steps for Feeling Good About Yourself," "My Mind Is Focused and I Am Ready to Learn") and teachers ("Plan to be Positive"). She likes to use lots of charts with words, since distractible students' eyes may wander and looking at the chart gives them another opportunity to read and learn.

Use bulletin boards to list classroom rules and behavior progress. Having rules posted (preferably on bright posterboard with large block letters that can be easily seen from the back of the room) can reduce the need to repeat the rules verbally. You can just point to the rule. For example, talking rules might be designated with a visual signal. Periods of open talking, low-voice talking, and no talking can be prompted through the use of signs showing either a "green light," "yellow light," or "red light," respectively. When the red sign is up and a student talks, teachers can refer to the sign without having to continually repeat the current limits on talking.

Behavior and assignment charts are also good tools for letting students monitor their own progress. These charts serve to remind students of the program, and help remind teachers to be consistent, too! Charts can be public or private. Many students respond better to private feedback on a small progress chart or checklist kept at their desk. This may be especially true for students who are having trouble. Public reminders may advertise their lack of success and lead to rejection, reduce self-esteem, and make the problem worse.

ASSISTIVE EDUCATIONAL TECHNOLOGY

New advances in educational technology can increase attention to tasks and students' connection to learning material. More and more classrooms are equipped with electronic visual aids. The interactive whiteboard projects computer-generated information onto a large screen for children to see. This technology may be especially helpful for students with ADHD because it can provide an unlimited array of diverse and captivating visual examples on any topic (as opposed to overhead projectors, which are limited to information generated on individual overhead sheets). This also allows for interactive capability where students can actively participate. A document camera can project book pages, which greatly sharpens the focus on material and allows for modeling the writing process and test-taking strategies. Many classrooms are also equipped with technology to improve auditory presentation. Teachers can use a microphone in classrooms with a sound field and speakers to increase the clarity of their lectures.

Newly developed software programs, including those with text-to-speech capability (e.g., Kurzweil) and speech recognition programs (such as Dragon NaturallySpeaking), may be very helpful for students with ADHD and specific learning disabilities. Students with ADHD also often benefit from learning word processing programs early on to assist with their written reports. This is particularly helpful for those students with messy handwriting due to fine motor problems. These programs allow students to edit their own writing without going through the laborious process of rewriting an entire draft. They can also use visual formats such as tables to present material and programs like PowerPoint for class presentations. Researching topics on the Web and then downloading photographs and diagrams can greatly enhance students' excitement about learning new subject matter. And digital recorders are useful for students to dictate assignments and stories or record lectures.

ESTABLISHING ROUTINES

Students with ADHD thrive in the midst of structure and routine. Having a routine helps kids organize their behavior and can be a great tool for preventing problems. Take the time to explicitly teach class routines to your students.

ROUTINES TO START THE DAY

- ○ Have a regular time and place to turn in homework.

- ○ Review the schedule for the day.

- ○ Start right away with a fun and easy written task that students can complete at their desks. This can clearly mark the beginning of the school day and provide a more structured transition. The task might be a simple puzzle to solve, a sentence to complete or correct, or a question to answer.

- ○ Have students set goals for themselves at the beginning of each day: In one study, sixth-grade students set goals for their behavior and academic work and then monitored them at 15-minute intervals during a two-hour period. They earned rewards for accurate self-assessment and for achieving daily goals. There was improvement in on-task behavior and academic performance and a reduction of disruptive behavior. Use of graphs to set daily or weekly goals may be especially effective. Lynn McGauly, a third-grade teacher at Sunset Elementary School in San Francisco, California, starts the day by going over the daily agenda. Each student has a monthly calendar at his or her desk. McGauly previews upcoming events for the day, week, and month. She also has students set goals for themselves each day. Sample goals include: being safe on the playground, being responsible by completing work, and being respectful by using positive words with classmates.

Students write down their daily goal on their copy of the school calendar. Over the course of the school year, goals are modified and become increasingly tailored to the student's specific challenges. McGauly also writes down a personal goal for herself (e.g., remembering to give a 5-minute warning before transition times) and shares it with the class.

ROUTINES DURING THE DAY

- ➲ Have a schedule that you stick to. Post the schedule on the wall so that upcoming activities can be planned for. Pictures of the scheduled activities can be used for kindergarten students.

- ➲ Teach major academic subjects in the morning. Most kids (and teachers) are fresher at this time, which maximizes their learning and your energy and also allows for a range of natural activity reinforcers at the end of the day.

- ➲ Alternate between active and quiet activities and between lecture, cooperative learning groups, and individual seatwork. Allow students to move during and between lessons. Let them stand in the back of the room as long as you control the parameters.

- ➲ Alternate between high-interest and low-interest activities. Have kids rotate through activity centers. David Agler, a first- and second-grade teacher at the Child Development Center at University of California–Irvine (UCI–CDC), draws an analogy to circuit training by referring to this as the "station-to-station workout." He has students, working at their own pace, first complete the least desired activities and then move on to the more desired activities. Assignments or projects are checked before the student can go on to the next. Activities of the day are depicted on a "Job Board"—this is a magnetic game board with spaces, each of which is labeled with a task or activity that needs to be completed. Each child has a magnetic laminated piece with his or her name on it. As students complete each task, they move their magnetic names across the board. Tasks include: library, reading, workbook, phonics games, math jobs and so on. Students complete more difficult tasks first and can receive a bonus at the end.

- ➲ Have routines for daily activities, such as assigning and collecting work and making transitions between activities. Consider using charts that list the steps for various routine activities. Then have students review the steps before each activity. Such routines help students with ADHD stay organized and focused on the task at hand.

⮑ Have routines for beginning and ending lessons. Set clear learning objectives—describe the topic to be covered and what students are supposed to learn. The lesson might begin with a review of related topics previously covered followed by new content. Also set clear behavioral expectations, so students know how they are supposed to behave during the lesson. This might include immediate praise (or stickers) for students showing readiness to learn by having their pencil out and looking at the teacher. At the end of the lesson, check for understanding.

⮑ Teach students what to do when they complete their work early. Post a list called "Things to Do When You're Done." The list might contain ideas about things to read, draw, design, make, and write. You might also consider having students start their homework when they have finished their classwork. To facilitate independence, homework assignments can be posted in the classroom each day. Students check the homework board and then get started on any of the assignments. Having students start homework during school allows them to ask questions when they don't understand something.

⮑ Carefully teach what to do when rotating between centers. Model exactly what students are supposed to do during the transition from one center to the next and then have them practice. Reward good transitions (e.g., give table points, exchangeable for small rewards, to students sitting at tables that rotate successfully).

⮑ Allow regular stretch breaks. Students with ADHD often become restless. When you notice this has happened, give the student an errand to run or a chore to do to expend the "excess" energy. They'll benefit from the break from sitting.

SET CLEAR LEARNING OBJECTIVES— DESCRIBE THE TOPIC TO BE COVERED AND WHAT STUDENTS ARE SUPPOSED TO LEARN.

■ ■ ■

ROUTINES TO END THE DAY

➲ Review how well students met their daily goals. In McGauly's class, each student evaluates how they did on their goal for the day. They rate themselves a on a scale of 1–3 and write it on their calendar. They discuss (with partners or table mates) successes and challenges meeting their goals and how their behavior affected the success of the activity they were doing (e.g., if a student had success with a target of getting started right away on an assignment, it might have helped him or her complete the assignment in time and earn free time). McGauly encourages a focus on the positive, and she keeps a compliment list on the front board to acknowledge students showing "goal behavior."

➲ Assign homework or review previously assigned homework. The assignment should be written down and reviewed verbally. Ask students questions to make sure they understand the assignment and which materials need to go home.

➲ Use a regular system for packing up materials and homework to go home. A checklist may be helpful. Do I have my homework, books, notes from school to take home, lunchbox, jacket, backpack?

➲ End the day on a positive note: Have students give themselves positive self-statements such as "I worked hard and met my goal" or "It was tough today, but I will try harder tomorrow."

DELIVERING LESSONS TO MAXIMIZE ATTENTION

You are competing with external stimuli (other kids, distractions in the room) and internal stimuli (daydreams, thoughts about things outside class) whenever you are teaching. Capture your students' attention through interesting, well-planned, and well-paced lessons.

➲ Present your group lessons in a creative and engaging way. The more you can do this, the better attention and behavior you will see from your students.

➲ Use language students can relate to. Use real-life examples that have meaning for them. Try to incorporate current fads (clothes, toys, games, food) and activities (playing soccer, going to the arcade) into your lessons.

- Bring life to your lecture. Try giving lectures as if you were a storyteller— raise and lower your voice, speed up and slow down your delivery, take on the role of a character in your lecture, and "ham it up" for a short while.

- Make sure that the most important points of your lecture are the most interesting. Say these points in a louder voice. Write them on the board in vibrant colors.

- Repeat what you say several times. This increases the chance that those with fleeting attention will hear it at least once.

- Keep long, complex sentences to a minimum. Students with ADHD usually have deficits in working memory and often in sequencing, so they simply can't maintain and process long strings of information at one time.

- Use demonstrations rather than straight lecture. Remember that "a picture is worth a thousand words."

- Give students many opportunities to respond. Research shows that the more opportunities students are given to respond the more they are engaged in the lesson.

- Use a variety of methods: Ask questions about the content and call on individual students for responses. In classes where only a few students raise their hands, make sure to call on everyone. Ask guiding questions: What is being asked? What information do you need? What operation do you use? To promote self-confidence, ask quiet students questions you think they will know the answer to or give inattentive students prompts that a question is coming. These might be in the form of an "attention check": "Okay, everyone, I am going to ask an attention check—Sacramento is the capital of California. . . . Attention Check! Sophie, what did I just say?" To avoid calling on the same student every time, some teachers use wooden craft sticks with student names and pull a stick to determine which student to call on. Also, use nonverbal (thumbs up or down) or whole-class/choral responses, or have students write down answers to questions on note cards.

- Look around your class while you are teaching. If an ADHD student is drifting off, redirect and involve that student. If the student is listening, reinforce that behavior.

- Encourage questions from students. The more actively they are involved in the material being presented, the greater their attention to task.

- Keep the noise level low, insisting that students raise their hands to speak.

- Use hand gestures when teaching. The types of hand gestures most helpful are called representational and deictic. Representational gestures imitate the shape or motion of objects (e.g., demonstrating what one is supposed to do with an object). Deictic gestures are pointing movements intended to provide direction and attract attention (e.g., pointing to a certain part of a puzzle). Research shows that children with ADHD focus longer on puzzle tasks and are more successful in completing them when representational and deictic hand gestures are used to teach and scaffold the task (Wang, Bernas, & Eberhard, 2004). The use of gestures may be especially helpful for students with ADHD because speech alone may not be sufficient to gain and sustain their attention to the task. Hand gestures often provide more concrete and accurate information than speech alone and are often more dynamic and captivating.

Besides using the techniques discussed above to keep lessons moving along swimmingly, there are a couple of other important things you can do to keep students with ADHD, and all students, firmly on course.

Scaffold learning. You can do this by providing cues to match the ability level of the student. This is especially important for difficult tasks involving new learning or when ability is low. Hand gestures, as described above, appear to be particularly effective. Other examples of scaffolding include use of verbal prompts such as questions, providing encouragement, verbally going through the steps of a task, using mnemonics, and modeling the thinking process to approach the task. Physical scaffolding might include the use of checklists, "cheat sheets," and demonstrations to break large tasks into smaller steps.

Keep the classroom rhythm. It is critical to consider both ability and attention span when planning lessons. A lively, fast pace is key.

- Keep lessons short. During didactic group instruction, length of attention span is often at its lowest, sometimes limited to five minutes or less. During individualized (one-on-one) instruction,

THE USE OF GESTURES MAY BE ESPECIALLY HELPFUL FOR STUDENTS WITH ADHD BECAUSE SPEECH ALONE MAY NOT BE SUFFICIENT TO GAIN AND SUSTAIN THEIR ATTENTION TO THE TASK.

■ ■ ■

attention span usually increases quite a bit and hands-on or experiential learning tasks can capture an ADHD student's attention for much longer. Take note of how long a particular student can stay on task and time your lessons accordingly.

➲ Limit downtime during a lesson. Students with ADHD often have difficulty waiting patiently while teachers are hunting for materials or making last-minute copies. It is at these times that minor disruptions can turn into major disruptions and make it difficult to settle the class down. Have all of your materials organized in advance to reduce teaching lag time. Keep your lesson very well organized. Prepare your lesson plan ahead of time and write an outline of your lesson on the board or use an overhead projector or interactive whiteboard. Stick to your outline.

➲ Limit downtime between lessons and periods. Transitions are notoriously difficult for students with ADHD. Teachers can easily spend up to a quarter of class time managing transitions between activities. To minimize transition time, it is best to make rules and consequences for transition clear (e.g., follow teacher directions, move quietly, keep hands and feet to yourself). Give clear signals as to the beginning and ending of a period and also give warnings for transition from one activity to another. Rather than say, "It's time to stop working," say: "One more minute to finish the problems, then it will be time to stop." Engage students in activities while they wait for the others to finish transitioning (e.g., have younger students imitate your hand-clapping rhythm, talk to older students about interesting current events).

➲ Have students who need a break run an errand. This can help them settle down and get to work.

➲ Some students respond well to using fidget toys or calming manipulatives when they are frustrated (squishy ball). These can be kept at their desks as long as the toy does not become distracting.

PEER-TO-PEER LEARNING

Peer-mediated approaches, such as peer tutoring and cooperative learning, can be particularly effective ways to teach students since these approaches encourage them to be actively involved in the learning process. Their involvement heightens their attention to and interest in the task, facilitating a high state of learning readiness.

PEER TUTORING

In classwide peer tutoring programs, all students are paired for tutoring with a classmate (DuPaul & Stoner, 2003). Students are first given training in the rules and procedures for tutoring their peers in subjects such as reading, math, or spelling. Then, during actual peer tutoring sessions, the tutor reads a script of problems to the tutee and awards points for correct responses. They then switch roles, with the tutee becoming the tutor and vice versa. During these tutoring periods (which are about 20 minutes in length), the teacher walks around the class to make sure the program is being implemented properly and to provide assistance, if needed. Bonus points can be awarded by the teacher to pairs who are following all of the rules. As an incentive, pairs can compete to see who can earn the most points. Studies have found that classwide peer tutoring enhances on-task behavior and academic performance of children with *and* without ADHD in general education classrooms—making it a useful approach for all students. Students with ADHD seem to have an easier time learning from a peer, and students without ADHD get practice teaching the skills, which solidifies their understanding of the material. **Note**: Peer tutoring is probably most effective for students with ADHD when they are paired with well-behaved and conscientious classmates. Careful training for students in the how-to of this approach is also important.

Many teachers use peer tutors called "Study Buddies" specifically to help students with ADHD develop better study and organizational skills. The buddy helps the ADHD student do things such as write down assignments, get homework in the backpack, and keep the desk area organized. To avoid social stigma, you may wish to pair all students in your class (with selective pairings of organized with less organized students). Then, instruct pairs to work together and help each other with organizational tasks. It is also a good idea to set up occasions for students with ADHD to be in the position of helping their classmates in areas of strength for them (e.g., putting together a project, reviewing math facts, practicing sports skills, reading to younger students). The tutoring role can be a great self-esteem booster.

PEER MONITORING

Having students monitor their peers' behavior can actually bolster areas of weakness for the student doing the monitoring. For example, one teacher finds that having a child who interrupts a lot keep track of those who are raising their hands greatly reduces the student's interruptions. With training and supervision, students can also learn to monitor peers' behavior at times like recess, when adult supervisors are in shorter supply. Cunningham and colleagues (2001) developed a student-mediated conflict resolution program in which peers serve as playground monitors. This program was found to reduce playground violence and negative interactions. However, several cautions are in order: Watch out for peer pressure and rejection and never have children administer punishment programs—studies show that having children correct the negative behavior of their peers can exacerbate the problem. If you do have peers serve as monitors, they should be carefully trained and supervised to ensure that students are accurate in their monitoring of behavior.

COOPERATIVE LEARNING

A very powerful way to involve peers in the learning process is through cooperative learning groups. Keep in mind, however, that cooperative learning requires that children work together in a manner in which all make contributions and get along. Many students with ADHD have trouble working in groups with other children. They may dominate the group or annoy their peers with silly, inappropriate behavior. They may unintentionally hurt the feelings of group members by making fun of their contributions. Particularly for students with ADHD cooperation needs to be taught. Start with very small groups or pairs and, as with peer tutoring, make a point of pairing children with ADHD with compatible peers. You might try assigning specific jobs to each student (one person to write down contributions of group members, another to get needed materials for the group, a third who calls on group members for contributions). Set rules for the groups, such as that everyone needs to participate and support one another. Have students role-play examples of following the rules and not following the rules. Then, during the cooperative learning period, walk from group to group and monitor students. At the end of the period, have kids evaluate how well their groups worked (What did we do well? What can we do better next time?). After students are successful working in pairs, you can increase the size of the groups to three or four children. Research shows that cooperative goal structures in learning situations (as opposed to competitive, individualistic goals) can facilitate both academic and social success. Activities that involve the group working together to achieve a product or tangible goal coupled with specific training in skills for working together is likely to lead to the most successful outcomes (Mikami, Boucher, & Humphreys, 2005).

PROMOTING PEER ACCEPTANCE AND SUPPORT

Peers often form opinions about their classmates based on how the teacher interacts with the child. All too often, this means that children form judgments about their ADHD classmates in the context of having seen the student reprimanded regularly for negative behavior. Don't ostracize anyone in your class. This can cause students to marginalize those with ADHD. Instead, set the stage for peer acceptance and support of all children. Promote a safe environment where students can participate without fear of giving the wrong answer (as long as it is not intentionally silly) and being ridiculed or embarrassed.

Teach children to support one another when they are doing well. Use group cheers for good work or behavior. Reinforce compliments. Peers can be wonderful motivators for success. One way to promote peer support is to actively teach acceptance of diversity. Deanne Zyromski teaches her first-grade students at Ruckersville Elementary School in Ruckersville, Virginia, that everyone has gifts and challenges. She likes to read books on children who have a wide variety of challenges, including ADHD, with a focus on helping students to appreciate one another's differences and strengths. She uses the phrase "No one can be you as well as you can be you." She encourages her students to think broadly about strengths and to value what each person can do—for example, skills such as drawing, throwing a ball with good aim, or building a Lego structure. Zyromski notes that cooking skills are great to highlight as strengths: e.g., the boy with leg braces who makes the best cocoa or the girl who is great at peeling potatoes. Showcasing each student's strengths can create a classroom where students focus on what each person can do, instead of what someone can't do.

Promotion of strengths can also be taught in the context of specific learning tasks. Two methods for this include multiple-ability instruction and assigning competence to low-status students. In multiple-ability instruction, teachers make clear that each task requires multiple abilities— no one has all the skills and we all have some of the skills. The second method involves the teacher watching for instances in which low-status or low-performing students, often those with ADHD, do well on an aspect of a task (e.g., observing astutely, making creative suggestions). The teacher then provides very favorable, specific, accurate, and public evaluation of this student's skills so that higher-status group members will hear and accept the teacher's evaluation. The teacher's feedback also includes the relevance of the ability to the task at hand so that peers will value the student's skills.

Research suggests that children who feel connected and safe in their school and classrooms are more likely to be academically and socially successful. There are a number of universal classroom intervention programs currently being used in school districts across the country with a focus on improving connections between school and students. Although the programs are not specific to the needs of students with ADHD, some include components which may be helpful for them. Positive Action and Caring School Community are two such programs aimed at improving school climate and character development; their methods, backed by research, show positive effects on the behavior of general education students. In the case of Positive Action, research also shows a positive effect on academic achievement (What Works clearinghouse).

CURRICULA FORMATS TO ENHANCE ATTENTION

One of the most powerful predictors of behavior in the classroom is the interest value of the curriculum to students. Children, those with and without ADHD, are naturally drawn to creative, novel, and captivating presentation formats. The extent to which you can design curriculum to include these elements will greatly enhance your success with ADHD and general education students. Remember to be flexible. Take advantage of as many teachable moments as you can. Interesting curricula include the following elements:

- ⮑ **Using multisensory approaches:** Present concepts visually, auditorally, and kinesthetically. Kids often remember concepts best when they are presented in many different ways. Have students read about it, hear about it, and act it out. Use chants and songs or jump rope while spelling new words.

- ⮑ **Using manipulatives rather than paper-and-pencil tasks:** Teach math facts using games and coins. Practice money skills by having students give change at a class store. Have them learn measurement skills by building something. Keep a stock of art supplies (clay, paints, markers) on hand for this purpose.

➲ **Emphasizing experiential learning and individualized projects in areas of interest and strength:** Jay Teeman has his fifth-grade students at Roscomare Road Elementary School in Los Angeles, California, select something they know how to do and teach it to the rest of the class. He gives students a list of things they can explain, such as making something to eat, performing a magic trick, demonstrating how to play a sport, or showing how to design something like a T-shirt logo. Students pick an activity and briefly explain the process using visual aids. Popular experiential learning units include those focused on development of daily living or life skills. Multiple subjects, including math, reading, social studies, and science, can be incorporated into lessons, which can involve activities in which students learn to keep checkbooks, decide on careers, make major purchases, find apartments, read want ads, and learn the pros and cons of many other real-life activities (going to the gym, having a pet, taking out a loan, buying insurance).

➲ **Using high-interest material:** Of course, interesting subject matter is critical. However, just a little spice sprinkled into somewhat dull material can add a spark of interest. Use games during lessons. For example, Zyromski modifies the "four-corners" game to teach a variety of concepts (each corner represents directions, or words, or math problems, and so on) to her first graders. Board games can be fun for teaching reading comprehension, phonics, and math computation. Computer games are also useful for drill and practice of skills in a variety of academic areas. Even adding interest value to materials can help. Use colored sheets of paper and colored chalk; underline in colors; use handouts that are presented in a visually interesting way.

➲ **Using high-interest content:** Cooking and food projects can be particularly captivating. Hands-on math and science projects (e.g., AIMS science activities) and most lessons with a participatory component are recommended.

➲ **Minimizing rote memorization**

➲ **Using computerized learning programs with self-correction built in:** ADHD students' attention is captured by interesting, interactive computer programs in a way that is often hard to duplicate in class. Research studies have shown that computer-assisted instruction can improve engagement and math performance in children with ADHD relative to written assignments (Ota & DuPaul, 2002).

➲ **Being enthusiastic yourself about the curricula!**

WRITTEN ASSIGNMENTS AND SEATWORK

Written work is often the weakest academic area for the ADHD student. Fine motor problems, poor planning of motor responses, and difficulty shifting attention from one activity to another make tasks such as copying, note taking, and giving written responses to readings a real challenge. Attention span is particularly important to consider when planning written assignments. Lengthy, repetitive work is usually difficult for the ADHD student. It requires much more effort on the part of an ADHD student to sustain the attention necessary to complete repetitive work than other students. When faced with columns of math problems or lengthy reading assignments followed by a barrage of questions, students with ADHD often give up. If they do attempt the task, they often take much longer to complete the work due to frequent lapses of attention.

To better sustain effort over time and motivate work completion, consider the following:

1. Break one large task down into several components. For example, instead of giving the student a big packet of work to complete for the day or week, give the student one page at a time.

2. Use a checklist of each step or task, and as it is completed, have the student check it off. The student can sign the bottom of the sheet and turn it in along with the assignment.

3. Limit the amount of work on each page to only a few problems or activities so it doesn't seem so overwhelming and cluttered. Cover up portions of the page not being used. Similarly, keep directions brief and clear.

4. Use worksheets that are clearly typed in large bold print.

5. Allot extra time to complete assignments and tests. Numerous studies show that children with ADHD process information more slowly and are slower in completing written tasks, despite understanding the concepts. The extra time enables students to demonstrate their knowledge without being penalized for attention lapses or their difficulty sustaining effort during complex learning tasks.

6. Use a timer. Give students challenges to complete their independent seatwork in a certain period of time—three minutes may be a good start for those especially weak at sustaining attention. Many students are motivated to "beat the clock"—and, as a result, are better able to sustain their attention to get through a task. Fran Martin also likes to use the timer for kids who rush through their work. She sets a minimum amount of time to work on a task in order to slow them down!

7. Give work breaks. Paying attention for long periods of time is tiring for students with ADHD. Work breaks that allow physical movement (stretching, standing, running an errand) may help some students become more efficient when they are working.

8. Allow students to type their reports on a word processor or tape-record lessons. Use of such strategies enables students to focus their learning effort on subject content rather than getting caught up in details not necessarily relevant to the task at hand. Note that many students with ADHD have fine motor difficulties, making this accommodation especially useful.

9. If you can, correct students' work as they do it. David Agler finds this practice very effective for his students. They receive a star on their page if the work is complete and correct or check marks by what needs to be adjusted. He ensures 100 percent accuracy and completeness by having students correct mistakes before they go on to the next activity. If you find it too time consuming to check everyone's work, just check the students who need the extra help. In general, students will learn much more if you give them feedback about their work as soon as they finish it.

10. Use highlighters or highlighting tape to distinguish what's important from what's not. Highlight key words or symbols. Color-code letters in difficult-to-spell words (e.g., *receive*).

NUMEROUS STUDIES SHOW THAT CHILDREN WITH ADHD PROCESS INFORMATION MORE SLOWLY AND ARE SLOWER IN COMPLETING WRITTEN TASKS, DESPITE UNDERSTANDING THE CONCEPTS.

■ ■ ■

11. Minimize writing on tasks emphasizing specific concepts and knowledge. For example, use web diagrams for categorizing and learning concepts.

12. Give students a choice about the order in which assignments or tasks can be done. Research shows that student choice reduces inappropriate behavior.

13. Teach students to proofread their work and correct their own mistakes. Make a list of common errors (misreading computation signs in math, omitting words in a story) and have students find their own!

14. Reduce the length of the written assignment to match students' attention spans. For example, have ADHD students complete every other math problem, or require fewer copies of spelling words. If you do choose to reduce the assignment, make sure the students' understanding of the material is not compromised by their doing less work. Only reduce repetitive or practice work after the concept has been mastered. But, even then, be careful. Some students may be more motivated and successful with shortened assignments, but others may come to expect less from themselves if they are given much shorter assignments. Their self-esteem may suffer if they don't think they can accomplish what their classmates can. Therefore, it is wise to focus your efforts on teaching the students to complete as much work as they can by using strategies such as increased incentives and positive feedback.

15. Teach students to give themselves encouraging self-statements. For example, before starting an assignment, they might say: "I know this will be hard, but I am going to keep trying. If I get stuck I will ask for help."

TESTS

Students with ADHD often have difficulty taking tests. They may learn the material but have a hard time reproducing it on an exam. To address this problem, teach your students these test-taking strategies.

1. Use study sheets completed during class lecture or independent work period and checked by you for accuracy. Study sheets may be fill-in-the-blank, short answer, or matching words to definitions and are to be used as guides for studying for tests.

2. Model frequent underlining and highlighting of main points.

3. Help students make up flash cards for each concept or idea. Play memory games with the flash cards.

4. Show students tricks to remember facts. For visual learners, have them tie concepts with mental images. For verbal learners, have them tie concepts with mnemonics.

5. Give practice tests and provide feedback to students.

6. Use interactive Web sites for test practice—these provide immediate feedback, and using the computer has extra interest value.

7. Allow students to take tests in a quiet, low-distraction area (e.g., a cubicle).

8. Allow use of multiple modalities to test knowledge. The written modality is most widely used, but it's also the area of greatest challenge for many children with ADHD. Consider allowing oral presentations and projects to test knowledge. Often, this is where students with ADHD can shine! Make it more interesting by letting kids use a microphone when they give an oral report.

9. Give extra time, if needed. Timed tasks may not allow students to show what they know.

10. Monitor students as they take the test to make sure they are reading the directions and doing the right problems.

11. Teach tricks for multiple-choice exams: crossing out wrong answers and other strategies for narrowing choices, not leaving any item blank, learning how to fill in Scantrons and how to match test items with Scantron items, and so on.

12. Post test dates on school Web sites.

TEACHING ORGANIZATIONAL AND STUDY SKILLS

A common and very frustrating experience for students with ADHD, their teachers, and their parents is to find that work was completed but it was the wrong assignment. Organizational and study skills are usually the problem, and these can and should be taught to students with ADHD. They usually need explicit guidance with these skills. As a first step, have students complete a self-assessment of organizational skills (if your assessment does not match theirs, explain your reasoning).

CHILD SELF-ASSESSMENT

Do I have trouble finding my:

_____ school supplies (pencils, erasers, etc.)?

_____ books, workbooks?

_____ folders?

- Is my desk messy? _____

- Is my backpack messy? _____

- Do I have old food or trash in my desk or backpack? _____

- Do I have a hard time staying on task? _____

- Do I have a hard time finishing work on time? _____

- Is my planner well organized so I know where everything is? _____

There are many tricks to help improve organizational and study skills. Try some of the following:

➲ Teach students to use an organized planner or notebook: a three-ring notebook with dividers for each subject and a pouch containing lots of pencils and erasers works well. The planner or notebook should include:

- Homework Assignment Planner (see page 124); you can also add a column for in-class assignments
- Pocket folder to hold papers/tests until they are punched (it's better to have all papers punched before giving them to students)

- Pocket folder for work to be completed on one side and work to be turned in on the other side
- Color code for each subject
- Stack of extra paper

➲ Monitor use of the notebook every day. Students can typically learn this system, but without consistent reinforcement, they will fail to use it. Have students write down the following steps on an index card taped inside their notebook and lead them through each one. Leave a space for students to check off each item as it is completed. Such self-monitoring systems can be highly effective with students in middle school.

Did I turn in my homework assignment? _____

Did I write today's class and homework assignment and the due dates in my book? _____

Did I put away all returned papers and tests in the right place? _____

Did I put away all handouts and worksheets in the right place? _____

➲ Do periodic desk and backpack checks (at least weekly, preferably daily to begin with). Help students organize their belongings and throw out trash. Give rewards for a clean desk and organized backpack and for following directions during the clean-out time. Use a checklist: Are necessary items present? Are unnecessary items absent?

➲ Tape a file folder to the side of each student's desk to store worksheets/assignments with separate sections for complete and incomplete work.

➲ Teach note taking. Use an outline on the board or on a handout. Stick to it. Highlight key points by underlining, using different colors, and so on. Tell students the important points to write down. Give students a handout to make sure that they have all of the important ideas.

◌ Check students' notes. Give points for getting the main ideas. Let students make an appointment with you after school to catch up on their notes. Try assigning study buddies. The buddy can be called upon to check completeness of notes and can help fill in details. But make sure the buddy doesn't end up doing all of the work.

◌ Practice time estimation. It is not unusual for students with ADHD to believe an assignment will take less time than it actually does. Have them time themselves completing an assignment. They should save the results so that they can more accurately estimate time for completing future projects.

◌ Give students a checklist for preparing their work area:

   1. What materials are needed for the task?

   2. What materials do I have on my desk?

   3. What materials need to be added?

   4. What materials need to be put away?
   (to avoid distraction)

◌ Help students organize for long-term reports. Deficits in executive planning skills make it very difficult for students with ADHD to tackle long-term reports—without assistance, these reports may not get started until the day before they are due and may lack needed organization and detail. To circumvent this tendency, students with ADHD need explicit guidance in how to break down the report into smaller tasks, prioritize, and set deadlines. For example, the report can be divided into a sequence of sections which are completed one at a time over the course of several weeks. Each section would include a main idea as well as supporting details (e.g., What does the animal look like? Where does it live? What does it eat?). Students can use a checklist with the sections listed in the order in which they are to be completed, the materials and information needed for each, and the due date to be checked off when completed. Be sure to give positive feedback for completion of each part, not just for the finished product.

◌ Engage students in the process of thinking, planning, and troubleshooting. Ask them for their ideas: "How are you going to remember to stay on task until you finish your work?" "What can you do to make sure you have the correct assignment written down?" "You left out words in your narrative; what can you do to prevent that?" "What steps will you need to complete for your long-term report?" If needed, help students come up with solutions. Have them write down the solutions. Then check in with them later to find out if the solutions worked or if others are needed. Be proactive with these strategies—when you know of a high-risk situation, prompt students to find solutions to the problems beforehand!

➲ Hope Hartman, a third-grade teacher in Grand Island, New York, classifies practices in the following way:

PRACTICES TO AVOID	BEST PRACTICES
Messy classroom No set routines Too many things floating around the room Too many places for things to be kept; walls are overly decorated and too busy.	Organized classroom Routine is the same each day. Everything has a place and is in its place. Room is decorated in a visually pleasing and uncluttered way—including ample wall space between posters.
No mention of organization	Taking time to organize yourself and monitor students' organization daily
Things shoved into desks	From day one, pencils always put away
Multiple stacks of papers, materials, and books on tables and shelves	Before leaving, folders and books put back in place so they can be found the next day. No "bare-naked papers"; all papers find proper home Color-coded notebooks to correspond with subject Clean desk—keep supplies down, two-pencil limit, one glue stick

Several formal training programs have been developed to teach organizational skills to students with ADHD (Abikoff & Gallagher, 2008; Langberg, Epstein, Urbanowicz, Simon, & Graham, 2008; Evans, Langberg, Raggi, Allen, & Buvinger, 2005). What is distinctive about these programs is the level of explicitness in teaching the skills, which is so necessary for these students. Self-questioning techniques and checklists and strategies for homework management including use of daily assignment books like those described earlier are key components. As an example, the Challenging Horizons Program (CHP) was developed for those in grades 4 through 7 (Langberg et al., 2008). The program includes three components.

1. Organization of the following: book bag, binder, and locker. A checklist includes what is needed to keep each of these areas organized. Sample checklist items: Is there a section for each class in binder? Is the homework folder in front of binder with homework to be completed on the left side and homework to be turned in on right side? Are folders and papers secured by a three-ring binder with no loose papers? The student receives points for each item on the checklist and the points can be traded in for a gift card.

2. Accurate recording of homework and tests in a planner. Student records all assignments and tests each day and teacher signs to ensure accuracy. Students earn free time for accurate daily records.

3. Long-term planning for tests and projects. Students are taught to use a planner and how to organize their materials.

Outcomes for CHP include substantial gains in organizational skills and homework success.

TEACHING SOCIAL SKILLS

Children with ADHD are at great risk for being rejected by their peers. Just as teachers and parents find their behavior difficult to tolerate, so do other children. Children with ADHD tend to be intrusive, impatient, easily frustrated, easily bored, bossy, self-centered, insensitive to social cues, and not inclined to follow rules. Inattention and lack of concentration make it difficult for them to hold conversations. These characteristics do not win many friends. Yet most children with ADHD desperately want friends. Their repeated social failures can be devastating to them and their parents.

As a teacher, there is much you can do to improve the social behavior of your students with ADHD. You can work individually with students in need; however, your entire class is likely to benefit from direct instruction in social skills they can use during group lessons and at recess. Several of the character development programs mentioned previously can be helpful for creating school communities conducive to positive peer relationships. They also often include instruction in specific social skills conducted through class meetings and exercises. Teachers can also help their students learn to manage their emotions and communicate more effectively.

To help students learn to manage conflict, Deanne Zyromski tells her first-grade students that feelings are not good or bad, but how you behave when you are feeling a certain way IS important. She teaches them to use "I messages" when they are feeling sad or mad; for example: *I felt (tell how you felt) when you (tell what other person did). I want (tell what you want). I felt mad when you took the ball from me. I want you to give me my ball back.* I messages should be delivered with a calm tone of voice and good eye contact.

A model social skills training program for elementary-age students with ADHD has been developed at a school-based treatment program specifically designed for ADHD housed at University of California–Irvine's Child Development Center (UCI-CDC) (Fine & Kotkin, 2003). The most intensive version of the training program occurs in a day treatment program via daily one-hour sessions, but the program has been successfully adapted for implementation in weekly sessions within regular schools and in outpatient clinics (Pfiffner & McBurnett, 1997). The program is implemented as a formal class and teaches a number of specific sportsmanship skills that are often a problem for youngsters with ADHD. Students learn the skills and then practice using them during games. Students usually have no difficulty learning the skills; their greatest challenge comes in using the skills in "real-life" situations. This means that these students require lots of practice and feedback before they are able to use the skills routinely. The model can also be used to address classroom issues during cooperative learning activities. Here are steps for running a social skills lesson.

➲ **Select an important skill to work on.** Skills that are common problems for children with ADHD include following activity rules, participating and staying with an activity, taking turns, cheering on others, cooperating, helping, sharing, tolerating frustration and accepting when things don't go the way they would like, being assertive, ignoring provocation, and solving problems. Work on one of these skills at a time. The amount of

YOU CAN WORK INDIVIDUALLY WITH STUDENTS IN NEED; HOWEVER, YOUR ENTIRE CLASS IS LIKELY TO BENEFIT FROM DIRECT INSTRUCTION IN SOCIAL SKILLS THEY CAN USE DURING GROUP LESSONS AND AT RECESS.

■ ■ ■

time spent on each skill will depend on the needs of your class. Changing "target" skills every week or two may best maintain student interest. You can always rotate back through skills that need more work after you have covered several others.

↪ **Introduce the "skill of the week" to students in an animated and brief didactic fashion.** One of the most valuable aspects to social skills training is developing a common vocabulary to describe the skills. Clearly identify the skill by saying, for example, "We are working on cooperation." Then review how, when, and why to use it. Actively involve the students (especially the children with ADHD) in the discussion. You may want to use a group challenge game to reinforce participation. For example, give tokens (e.g., "good sports bucks") to children who participate in the discussion. If the class earns a certain number of "bucks," they get to pick a game of their choice to play at the end.

↪ **Model the skill of the week.** You should demonstrate both the right and wrong way (kids usually enjoy seeing their teacher do it the wrong way!).

↪ **Have students role-play the positive use of the skill in selected situations.** Give kids brief scripts to follow, such as joining an activity, letting someone else have a turn to talk or perform a task, responding to a request to play, leaving a game, or responding to teasing. After each role-play, have students evaluate one another. For example, a thumbs up means the student did a good job and used most of the targeted social skills, a medium thumbs (parallel to the floor) means the student used some of the skills but left out an important one, and a thumbs down means the student didn't use the skill. Students should share why they gave the ratings they did. Focus on the positive as much as possible. Let students redo role-plays that receive poor ratings. You should also be sensitive to students' feelings of rejection and exercise caution during these evaluations.

↪ **Have students practice the skills during group activities.** This can be during class time or during an already scheduled recess, PE class, or cooperative learning activity. Plan on about a 15-minute activity period. Just before the activity, have students predict how well they will do showing good social skills. You may want to use the "Goodsport Thermometer" (or call it the "Cooperation Thermometer" if you are doing this during a cooperative learning activity) described on page 56. Then, during the activity, give students immediate feedback regarding their use of the skills. You may want to provide tokens for kids showing certain social skills during the group activity.

⮑ **When the activity is completed, have students review their performance.** You can have them match their ratings with the teacher evaluation using the students Goodsport Thermometer. Have students tell you what went well and what they could do to make it go even better next time.

⮑ **Reward students for using the skills taught.** This also promotes group cohesion. For example, offer a group party (e.g., popcorn party) when the class meets a specific goal over a period of time. To track progress toward meeting the goal, you can use a large posterboard with a picture of the reward (in this case, a bag of popcorn) and a place to put stickers (or kernels, for this goal) they are earning toward the reward. Students can earn stickers either individually or as a group for showing the "social skill of the day (or week)." Once all of the stickers (or in this case, kernels) have been earned, the class gets the popcorn party.

⮑ **Periodically reward the class throughout the day for showing the social skill of the week.** This way you will increase use of the skills across the entire day. You can put up posters depicting target skills, have adults wear badges with the skill written on it, or give students badges or tickets for showing the target skills, which can be traded for weekly raffles. You can also encourage students to look for examples of the skills being exhibited by other children or adults in other settings. For an individual student with more severe social deficits, you might also want to institute an individual token economy or school-home report card targeting specific areas of concern for that child. Also, be aware that most children with ADHD do not generalize these skills to other group settings (e.g., recess, home, after-school programs, team sports) on their own. They need coaching and reinforcement for good social skills in all settings. Therefore, it is recommended that you send home a list of the social skills you are working on in class and examples of each skill. That way, parents can reinforce the skills at home and help their child generalize what was learned in class.

USING THE GOODSPORT THERMOMETER

A "Goodsport Thermometer" is a visual aid developed by the staff at the UCI-CDC school for helping kids set goals and evaluate their own behavior. The Goodsport Thermometer has a 5-point rating scale to monitor the presence or absence of good sport behavior during games. Higher scores mean more good sport behavior. For exceptional good sport behavior by all students, the thermometer goes above 5 and "breaks." This can be easily adapted to other behavior goals; for example, a "Cooperation Thermometer" or an "On-Task Thermometer."

You can use the Goodsport Thermometer in a variety of ways and for a variety of purposes. Try the following (Agler, 1995) ideas:

- Prompt students to think about good sport behaviors before the game (e.g., "What do you think we have to do to get a five on the Goodsport Thermometer during freeze tag?"). Have kids predict how well they think they will do right before they start a game.

- Make a Goodsport bulletin board displaying the thermometer to monitor students' progress each day. Go over progress with the class (e.g., "When we get a five on the Goodsport Thermometer we mark it on the chart. Look how many fives we have scored!").

- After the game is over, have students evaluate how they did and compare their ratings of the game with others (e.g., "I voted for a four for that game. Who matched with me? Why did you vote for a four?"). Use the teacher rating as the "gold standard."

- Have students explore the association between good sportsmanship and their feelings during games (e.g., "I noticed that most of you say you had fun on days when the class votes for a five on the Goodsport Thermometer!").

- Reward high ratings with group cheers and tokens such as Goodsport Bucks, exchangeable for group rewards. Prompt the positive alternative behaviors when the class earns less than a five (e.g., "What can we do next time to make our soccer game a five?").

Use the thermometer frequently at the beginning of the year (when the skills are first being learned and the class is still developing cohesion). Over time, you can fade its use. This procedure helps students learn quickly what is expected and rewarded during games and activities. Here is a sample social skills lesson.

LESSON TOPIC: ACCEPTING CONSEQUENCES

Teacher: Today we are going to talk about what you can do when something happens that you don't like or when things don't go your way. Let's say you are mad because someone called you out in a game. You know you should be out, but you are mad because you want to keep playing. Now there are a lot of things you can do. You can get really mad and start yelling at the person who called you out (*teacher models yelling*). You can get so upset that you start crying (*teacher models crying*). You can go to the coach and start whining about it (*teacher models whining*). All of these might be high-risk choices, though. What's wrong with these choices?

Jamal: You can get in trouble for fighting.

Lilly: You can lose friends. People won't want to play with you.

Osiris: You can get kicked out of the game.

Teacher: That's right. They're high-risk choices because they might get you in trouble. What would be a better choice?

Ahmad: Just go out.

Teacher: That's a good idea. In our class, that's called accepting. Accepting is when you keep on following the rules and getting along with others when something happens that you don't like or don't want. Let's talk about how you can show accepting. First, how do you think your body should look? Like this (*teacher clenches her hands*) or like this (*teacher models a calm body*)?

Osiris: Like the second time.

Teacher: That's right. You can show accepting by having a calm body posture. Arms and hands are by my side. My face is relaxed. Now how should I sound? Like this (*teacher loudly says: "It's not fair!! You're cheating!! I don't have to go out if I don't want to!"*) or this (*teacher calmly says: "Darn it, I wish I wasn't out"*)?

Ahmad: You should be like the second time: not yelling.

Teacher: That's right. Why do you think it is important to show accepting?

Jamal: You should show accepting because you will have more friends and the game will be more fun.

Teacher: When do you think you should show accepting?

Lilly: You should show accepting when you are called out, or when you don't get to do something you wanted to do.

Teacher: Those are good answers. Jamal, Lilly, Ahmad, and Osiris all earned participation points for their contributions. So you can show you are accepting by what you look like and what you sound like. Your body should look calm and your voice should be calm. Let's do some role-plays to practice accepting.

(*Teacher gives two students a brief script to follow that involves their being called out during a game of tag. They practice for a moment and then the teacher and the students do the role-play in front of the rest of the class.*)

Teacher: Mark and Susie, you were just tagged so you have to go to the sidelines.

Mark: (*frowns and sighs, but goes out*) Okay.

Susie: Okay. (*goes out*)

(*Afterward, the teacher has the class rate how well they showed accepting in the role-play.*)

Teacher: Okay, everyone rate Susie and Mark. Rate Susie with your left thumb and Mark with your right thumb. If you think they were accepting, give a thumbs up.

If you think they were mostly accepting, but left something out, give a medium thumbs. If you think they didn't show accepting, give a thumbs down. *(Students rate.)* Leslie, why did you give a thumbs up?

Leslie: Because I thought they went out right after they were called out and had calm bodies and calm voices.

Teacher: I thought so, too. Mark frowned a little bit, but that's okay as long as he doesn't yell or refuse to go out. Susie and Mark, you both showed all the parts of accepting. Good job. Here are your points for participation. *(Teacher gives instructions to the class for the upcoming game.)* The game you will be playing today is freeze tag. In this game, you will have lots of chances to show accepting. Before we play, let's have everyone make predictions on the thermometer. How do you think you will do? Do you think you're going to break the thermometer today with all of your good social skills?

Students *(in unison)* Yes!

Teacher: I hope you do, too! I'll be looking for accepting today. I'm also looking for good sports. Let's play. *(Game begins. Students show good accepting during the game.)*

(After the game is over, teacher concludes the discussion.)

Teacher: How do you think you did?

Students: We broke the thermometer!

Teacher: I saw a lot of accepting out there today. I agree! You broke the thermometer. That will be 100 extra Goodsport Bucks for the group! How did you like playing the game today when everyone was accepting?

Students: It was fun!

Teacher: It's usually more fun when everyone is accepting. Now remember, I'm going to be watching for accepting all week.

USING PROBLEM SOLVING

Many ADHD children respond impulsively and don't think about the many options they have for handling difficult situations. They act before thinking. One approach for changing this is to teach children how to solve problems—that is, teach them to think before acting. Students can be taught specific steps to solve problems.

I. What's the problem?

2. What are my choices?

3. Pick one.

4. Do it.

5. Did it work? If it did, pat yourself on the back. If not, go back to step 3.

Whenever a problem occurs, the student can signal the need to do a "problem solving" and the teacher can then guide the student through the problem-solving steps. The student should be told to think of at least three choices. One choice may be a high-risk choice, which means that it will probably lead to more problems. The others should be low-risk choices, which have a greater chance of a positive outcome. The student then selects one of the low-risk choices to do, does it, then evaluates how it worked. Here is an example.

I. What's the problem? Sean hit me.

2. What are my choices? Hit him back (high-risk choice), tell the teacher, walk away.

3. Pick one. Tell the teacher (not a high-risk choice).

4. Do it. (Eric tells the teacher who then tells the two boys to discuss the problem. The teacher tells Sean to sit out one game for hitting.)

5. Did it work? If it did, pat yourself on the back. If not, go back to step 3.

This approach gives students an opportunity to think carefully about what happened rather than simply react in the moment. Better solutions are the result. Take note: Students with ADHD often don't do problem solving on their own, even after learning the steps. They need lots of supervision and reinforcement to use this approach consistently. Although social skills training can be helpful in teaching appropriate skills, promoting dyadic friendships for students with ADHD has considerable value, especially for those who are socially isolated. Consider students in the class who might make good partners for the child with ADHD. Pair them for activities. Encourage interactions during recess. Suggest that parents to arrange play dates.

LOOKING BACK
A College Student's Perspective

An interview with Blake, diagnosed with ADHD, now an undergraduate at UC Berkeley (Taylor, 2007)

INTERVIEW

What accommodations helped you the most while you were going through school?
- Taking breaks
- Extra time
- Extra space for written work (e.g., on exams)
- Extra space in class to spread out and do work
- Visual reminders
- Using color in note taking
- Having an interactive class

What kinds of teachers helped the most?
- Teachers who noticed when I did well. I felt like I could succeed, that I was going somewhere, not just messing up.
- Teachers who did not humiliate—humiliation zaps motivation.
- Teachers who were understanding, strict but not austere, who would understand that my behavior was not intentional to be disruptive; it was impulsive, it wasn't the teacher's fault.
- Teachers who talked to me and became a friend.
- Small accommodations were a big deal, and having many teachers provide this was a huge reason for my success.

What is important for teachers to know about peers?
- Teachers, not students, should assign the groups—otherwise it's humiliating to be picked last.
- Teachers should help students be successful in front of their peers.

CHAPTER 3

BEHAVIOR MANAGEMENT BASICS

Even the best curriculum or most organized classroom environment won't be sufficient for effective teaching without a few key elements of classroom management in place. It's a short list, really—establish ground rules, involve students in lessons, use prompts, know when to parcel out praise and criticism—though it takes finesse and focus to implement.

ESTABLISHING AND IMPLEMENTING RULES

Involve students in generating the rules. On the first day of class, make a list of four or five rules using suggestions from students. Word rules in a clear, positive way. Wording in a positive way keeps students' attention focused on what they are to do, instead of what they are not to do. Here are some examples:

- Use quiet voices in the classroom.
- Walk, don't run, in the classroom and in the school.
- Use good manners.
- Line up quietly.

Write rules in large bold lettering on a large piece of construction paper. You can add pictures depicting each rule (especially with younger children). Assign each rule a number or color for easy reference later. Make sure students understand each rule. Have them give examples of rule-following behavior as well as rule violations. You and your students can sign the rules—the signatures would indicate that they understand the rules and are planning to follow them. Post rules in a place easily visible to all students.

Deanne Zyromski likes to solicit ideas for rules from the kids in her first-grade class. She discusses the reason for having rules as a group—to keep the class a safe place. Once she has about seven rules, she sums it up: Treat others like you would like to be treated. Then she explains that this one rule pretty much covers everything. Students and teacher sign the paper. She also posts a Norman Rockwell poster with the phrase: *Do unto others as you would have them do unto you.*

Simply establishing the rules will not guarantee that they will be followed. It is crucial that you show students clearly what to do and what not to do—that is, to demonstrate what exactly is following the rule and what is not. It is also essential in the beginning to review and practice the rules every day, and especially before each activity (after a couple of weeks, you can emphasize the rules less often). Have selected students give examples of following the rules. Then, throughout the day, you can insert "rule checks" while you teach. Praise individual students who are following one or more of the rules. It is especially important to notice when students with ADHD are following the rules, since they benefit from frequent feedback about their behavior. Here are some examples:

> "It's time for a rule check. I see Corinne is following rule number five and Ben is following rule number two. I see the entire first row has rule number three perfected!"

> "Hold on to that question and keep raising your hand, Nancy. I'll get to you in a minute."

If you notice one student not following a rule, point out those who are. This often motivates the student to follow the rule without ever having to give direct negative attention to the behavior. Be sure to comment on that child's behavior once it is "in line" with the rules.

HAND SIGNALS AND VISUAL PROMPTS

Kids often respond better to nonverbal prompts as opposed to verbal reminders (especially lengthy and repetitive verbal reminders). Have a signal for each rule. For example, if rules are numbered you can raise the number of fingers corresponding to the specific rule followed. Other examples include raising your fingers to your lips to signal quiet, raising your palm to signal stop, and shaking your head to signal no. One teacher likes to use hand signals in the shape of a C pressed against her mid-body—this signals the child to check their body and behavior. You can also give a V sign for victory when you see a rule being followed! Another signal is called the "quiet coyote" (pinky and pointer fingers are up and third and fourth fingers are touching the thumb), signaling that ears are listening and mouth is closed. David Agler uses a poster depicting a voice meter in his kindergarten and first-grade class to teach appropriate voice volume. The picture of the voice meter has settings demarcated for No Talking, Whisper Voice, Classroom Voice, Inside Voice, Playground Voice, or Outside Voice. He sets the voice meter by placing a movable arrow next to the appropriate "setting" before each activity for all students to see. Students are praised for keeping their voices within the selected level. If an individual student or the class becomes too loud, the voice meter serves as a reminder. Be consistent in enforcing the rules. Letting a child "get away" with rule violations even one time makes it harder for the student to follow the rule next time.

Using child-friendly analogies can make the learning process more fun. Agler teaches students to regulate their own behavior with their imaginary game controllers (inside their bodies). Students first think about what they are doing: Is my voice too loud? Am I in my seat? Then they use their imaginary video switches that make them shout, move, and so on, to lower their voices or calm their bodies.

INVOLVING STUDENTS IN LESSONS

One of the most beneficial things you can do to prevent problems and maximize learning is to *involve* students with ADHD. These kids thrive on interaction, and involvement in the lesson will make the difference between engagement and disengagement. Involving students (especially those with ADHD) should be an ongoing part of your teaching and should start right away. Whenever you sense students may be drifting off or becoming disruptive, pull them back in. Student involvement also allows you to perform ongoing student evaluation to see if more instruction is needed. Use the following strategies to involve students:

- **Check to see that the student is following along on the right page or giving you eye contact when appropriate.** Use physical prompts as necessary (point to the right page, move student's chair into the proper position).

- **Ask questions.** Call on students ("Who can tell me . . . ?") or have them respond in unison. Routinely check students' understanding of the lecture. Keep in mind that students with ADHD often require more time to respond to questions.

➲ **Encourage active responses during lessons.** Have students solve problems at the board and use movement to signal answers (e.g., thumbs up means yes, thumbs down means no). Have them play-act answers. Give students activity sheets to complete mid-point in a lesson or at the end. Vary the pattern.

➲ **Have the student with ADHD be a teacher's assistant during lessons and transitions.** Allow the student to turn pages, use a pointer, or get materials needed for your lecture or demonstration. Use the student's worksheet as an example for the class.

GIVING DIRECTIONS TO INCREASE COMPLIANCE

Directions may be given as a way to instruct during a lesson or as a way to manage behavior. Unfortunately, a short attention span, lack of inhibition, and distractibility all interfere with compliance. Noncompliance often results in teachers having to restate directions, sometimes repeatedly, with increasing frustration but little positive impact. To increase the likelihood that students with ADHD will listen to and follow your directions, use these guidelines for giving instructions to individual students.

1. Get students' attention, preferably with eye contact, before giving directions. Use a standard phrase or sign: "Stop, look, and listen."

2. Stand close to the student or students. Don't yell from across the room. This requirement is eased by having students with the most difficulty following directions seated close to you.

3. Be specific about what you want them to do.

4. Be brief.

5. Make a statement; don't ask a question. Precede your direction with the following: "You have a direction to . . . (go to your seat, get your book out, follow the quiet rule)."

6. When appropriate, give choices: "You have a math page and a science page to complete. Which would you like to do first?" "You can choose to continue drawing now or you can choose to clean up now. If you choose to clean up, you'll earn your recess. If not, you will have to sit out of the recess game and you will still need to clean up."

7. Give directions in the sequence in which they are to be completed.

8. Have the student repeat back the instruction to ensure understanding (e.g., "I asked you to clean up now. What are you going to do?"). One teacher with more than 30 students in her class found this to be the most important part about giving directions to her students with ADHD.

9. Use verbal prompts and visual cues to get started; walk the child through the first part of the assignment.

Use these guidelines for giving directions to groups.

1. Make sure everyone is quiet and is giving you eye contact.

2. Walk around the room to be sure students' attention is not compromised by fiddling with toys or writing notes to friends.

3. Keep the directions simple.

4. Use visual cues along with verbal directions. Write instructions on the board, or an overhead.

5. Walk students through the directions.

6. Ask for unison responses to repeat the directions.

7. Quiz students to ensure understanding.

Research in classrooms supports the effectiveness of minimizing repeated commands. Teachers of grades K–4 were trained to deliver commands with no more than one repetition. If the child did not comply, he or she was given a warning of a consequence. If compliance still did not occur, the consequence was issued. Teachers reported that reducing their repetitions of commands in this way significantly improved students' compliance in their classrooms (Kapalka, 2005). See the chart on the next page for specific problems and solutions (the Do's and Don'ts).

DO'S AND DON'TS FOR GIVING EFFECTIVE DIRECTIONS

Statement	Problem	Better
"Jason, would you collect all of the papers?"	Implies a choice	"Jason, please collect the papers."
"Okay, class. It's time to get back to work. Turn to chapter five of your book and you will find an experiment to do. All of the materials are on the back counter. Make sure to answer all questions on the worksheet. When you're done, turn in your worksheet. Then it will be time to start your math."	Too many directions at once	Give sufficient time, such as 5 to 10 seconds, to complete each step in between directions.
"I need everyone to show good behavior."	Too vague	Define good behavior: "I need everyone to sit properly, hands on desk, and show me your eyes. That way I know you are listening."
"Pleeeze! Be quiet!!!!!"	Too emotional	Stay calm: Use a nonverbal sign—turn off the lights, use a hand signal—to tell students it's time to be quiet.
"Why can't you ever listen the first time?"	Unanswerable question	Be direct: "You have a direction to listen the first time."
"Put all of your things in your desk."	The direction would work for most students but is too general for students with ADHD.	Give more specific directions and help students organize where their things should go.
"Do you want to lose your recess?"	A threat given in an emotional way can provoke many students with ADHD	"If you don't finish your work, you will lose your recess."
"Before you go to recess, you will need to finish your language arts assignment."	The order of tasks is not presented in the order in which they are to be completed and can pose difficulty for children with attention or working memory problems.	Present tasks in the order to be completed: "Finish your language arts assignment and then you can go to recess."

USING YOUR ATTENTION STRATEGICALLY

Using positive attention strategically is one of the most important teaching tools for the classroom. It means that you purposely use your positive attention to help students remain on task and redirect those who don't. When using positive attention strategically, you search for and attend to positive behaviors throughout the day (especially those you want to see more of). For students with ADHD, this means you may need to attend to behaviors that you ordinarily expect students to do without difficulty, such as getting started on assigned work, raising a hand to talk, or staying seated properly during a class discussion. Remember that students with ADHD usually need more frequent positive feedback than other students. Walking around the room and touching the students' shoulders or backs while they are working is a very helpful way to keep them on task. When minor behavior problems do occur, attend to and praise those students who are on task and ignore the off-task students. Those students are then likely to copy or model the students who were praised in an attempt to gain your attention as well. Remember to praise immediately once the problem student is back on task. Pay close attention to the high-risk situations for students with ADHD (individual seatwork, long or repetitive lessons, transitions between activities, unstructured times) and give extra praise at these times. See the next page for tips about giving praise.

A caveat, though: While ignoring is useful for some mild misbehaviors, immediate corrective feedback is required for more disruptive behavior. Your corrective feedback needs to be just as strategic as your positive feedback. Negative teacher attention can be reinforcing and can perpetuate the problem you are trying to correct. To use corrective feedback strategically, keep it immediate and brief. It is only one tool in the context of an otherwise positive, engaging instructional program (see page 71).

Keep in mind that positive behavior may not always present itself to you as dramatically as negative behavior. This makes it harder to keep up your rate of praise and you may end up interacting with students only when problems occur. To avoid this, you may need to give yourself reminders to praise more often. Some teachers find that posting a reminder sign (e.g., "Catch Them Being Good") in an area where they are liable to look helps. Whenever teachers look at the sign, they are reminded to praise. Some teachers like to keep track of their rate of praise. You might use a tally sheet for this. Another method is to store tokens in a clothing pocket. Each time you praise, move a token from one pocket to another. Set a goal of transferring all of the tokens by the end of the period or day.

> WHILE IGNORING IS USEFUL FOR SOME MILD MISBEHAVIORS, IMMEDIATE CORRECTIVE FEEDBACK IS REQUIRED FOR MORE DISRUPTIVE BEHAVIOR. YOUR CORRECTIVE FEEDBACK NEEDS TO BE JUST AS STRATEGIC AS YOUR POSITIVE FEEDBACK.

■ ■ ■

Don't expect that students with ADHD will change dramatically with the use of praise or ignoring inappropriate behavior. They typically need richer incentives to motivate positive behavior.

TIPS FOR PRAISING

Be specific. Label the behavior you like.

Say: "I like the way you followed directions right away," not just "Thank you."

Say: "You have done a great job completing all of those problems," not just "Good job."

Praise immediately when you see positive behavior.

If you wait, you may miss your chance or you may forget.

Praise that is focused on effort and not on intelligence or ability is best for improving motivation and persistence in challenging tasks.

Don't say: "You are so smart."

Say: "You really worked hard on that problem."

Research shows that those who receive ability-focused praise are more likely to become discouraged and give up on challenging tasks compared to those who receive effort-focused praise (Dweck, 2006). Children with a "growth mind-set" (they understand intelligence is malleable) feel empowered to take on challenges and are higher achievers than those with a "fixed mind-set" (they believe intelligence is static, and hence feel powerless in gaining skills/knowledge they don't already have).

Praise improvement.

Don't wait for heroic efforts or an "A" paper. Students with ADHD often benefit from praise for acts that other students do automatically. Notice the little things that are big things for students with ADHD.

Say: "You got your pencil and book out right away! You found the right page!"

Say: "You're being patient! You remembered to raise your hand! I noticed you completed that tough division problem."

Keep your praise free from put-downs and instructions, no matter how subtle.

Don't say: "You should always keep your desk that clean."

Say: "Your desk is spotless!"

Don't say: "Finally, you remembered your homework."

Say: "I like the way you remembered your homework today."

Be genuine and enthusiastic.

Don't count on perfunctory praise. Take the extra effort to walk over to the student and show your pleasure at his or her behavior. Make it a practice to publicly announce good effort and accomplishments. But, if you sense a particular student might be embarrassed by such attention, do it privately.

Praise often.

Students with ADHD need to hear positive feedback often. Try to set a goal of giving two to three praises to students with ADHD every hour. Even more important, keep the ratio of positive to negative feedback high. And while you should make a point to praise students with ADHD regularly, you also don't want to forget about your other students.

Teach students to self-administer praise.

Talk about the value of positive self-talk; for example, "I worked hard on that paper. It paid off!"

TIPS FOR IGNORING INAPPROPRIATE BEHAVIOR

Ignore behavior that is intended solely to get your attention.

Ignoring works well for whining, arguing, repeated complaints about the fairness of an established rule, and low-level non-disruptive misbehavior. It also works well for students who call out answers out of turn. If the goal of a student is to get out of working or following a direction or gaining the attention of peers, ignoring won't work.

Use active ignoring when you choose to ignore.

Purposely ignore misbehavior by not commenting on it and not looking at the student. Be consistent. Problems will increase if you ignore the behavior sometimes and then attend to it at other times. *Warning:* Ignored behavior may initially get worse. Have a plan to deal with this.

Stop ignoring the moment you see the student behaving properly.

Praise the good behavior immediately.

Never ignore aggressive or destructive behavior.

Use strategies for setting limits, discussed below. A time-out or a loss of privileges may be necessary.

TIPS FOR SETTING LIMITS

Choose your battles. If you commented on every instance of off-task behavior in your classroom, you would have little time left for instruction. Corrective feedback is generally not necessary for brief, non-disruptive off-task behavior. Prioritize those behaviors that may require correction. For example, which is more important: having the student stay seated during the entire lesson, or remembering to raise his hand before speaking? Pick one area to focus on. Once you have success in one area, you can go on to the next.

Use prudent feedback (Pfiffner, Barkley, & DuPaul, 2006). Prudent approaches stop problem behavior in its tracks; imprudent approaches can escalate problems to new heights. What is a prudent approach? It involves giving corrective or negative feedback in a brief, specific, and direct way. The feedback is given right after the negative behavior starts and every time the negative behavior occurs. It is also given in close proximity to the student and in a calm, matter-of-fact tone of voice. It is crucial that corrections are not delivered in an angry or hostile manner; otherwise, the student may miss the message and focus instead on perceived unfairness, becoming angry at the teacher and either fighting back or trying to avoid the teacher. See the chart below.

PRUDENT AND IMPRUDENT FEEDBACK	
Prudent (Best Practices)	**Imprudent**
Brian, why aren't you working?!	Brian, please get to work.
How many times do I have to tell you to stop talking? Other students can't concentrate when you are so loud. You know the quiet rule. You're going to have to learn how to follow it.	Stop talking or you will have to go back to your seat.
I told you before recess to clean up your mess. I noticed that you went to recess anyway. You have to remember to clean up before recess.	I gave you a direction to clean up. If you don't start right away, you will start losing recess time.

For persistent or more serious problems, loss of privileges, tokens, or other rewards may occur, or a time-out may become necessary. The prudent use of these consequences will be discussed beginning on page 110.

INTEGRATING INSTRUCTION, RULES, AND FEEDBACK TO PROMOTE GOOD ATTENTION AND BEHAVIOR

Basic methods to improve attention and behavior include: scanning the classroom, having students participate and stay involved, setting rules, giving clear directions, and using strategic praise and prudent corrective feedback. These methods should be sprinkled liberally throughout the lesson. Whether behavior is good or bad, attentive or off task, the teacher should insert frequent comments about attention and behavior while simultaneously delivering the lesson. These methods are for use with the entire class, although more frequent use will be necessary for students with ADHD. This approach may feel like an annoying interruption of your lesson plan, yet without these methods, good behavior goes unnoticed and negative behavior often escalates until it must be noticed. By that time, the behavior is more out of control and you will likely feel frustrated about having to stop teaching in order to reprimand students who are off task.

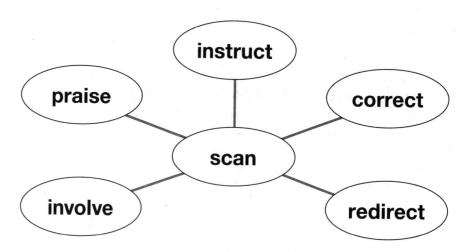

EXAMPLE 1: Here is how one teacher integrates verbal comments about behavior into her lessons. Look for the basic elements: scanning, involving students, setting rules, giving clear directions, and using strategic praise and corrective feedback.

Teacher: Let's review the stages of the life of the butterfly. Can anyone tell me what they are? (*scans class with careful attention to Bill, a student who has ADHD; notices that he is not paying attention and decides to involve Bill at this point so that he is more likely to tune in for the rest of the discussion*)

Teacher: Bill, (*waits briefly until he gives her eye contact, a sign that he is paying attention*) can you tell me the stages of life of the butterfly? (*involves student; gives clear directions*)

Bill: First there is an egg, then the egg turns into a caterpillar, then it spins into a pupa, then it turns into a butterfly.

Teacher: That's right. You remembered all four stages. I like the way you listened to the question and gave me good eye contact. That way I know that you are listening. (*strategic praise in a pleasant, non-accusatory tone*)

In this example, the teacher could have chosen to ask Bill for the answer without repeating the question or have reprimanded him for not listening. If either of these two options were selected, the teacher might have missed the opportunity to praise Bill for attending successfully. The ADHD student has had many years of being scolded for his misbehavior. By the time you have such children in your class, they may feel that they can't be successful. Your job is to teach them that they can be successful.

EXAMPLE 2: While talking about government in Texas, the teacher scans the class every minute or so to see if everyone is attending. During a scan, she notices that Sui is trying to show his neighbor, Justin, a toy from home. Justin has not yet directed his attention to Sui. She walks over to Sui, who fortunately is sitting near her.

Teacher: I like the way Justin is paying close attention. (*strategic praise*) Justin, can you tell me the capital of Texas? (*While talking, she opens her hand to Sui without saying a word. Sui puts the toy in her hand.*)

Justin: Austin.

Teacher: *(still standing next to Sui)* Good listening, Justin. *(strategic praise)* Sui, no toys during class. I need your eyes and ears on me. *(prudent corrective feedback; lesson continues)*

Here, the teacher could have told Sui to put the toy away from across the room and scolded him for playing. She also could have waited a few seconds to see if Justin would respond. The timing on this intervention was critical. She stopped the problem because she caught it very early. It helped having the high-risk child right by her so she could watch his every move. She also minimized what she said to Sui, saving him from public embarrassment. Removing the toy prevented future disruptions.

EXAMPLE 3: In this model, we see how a teacher handles calling out in class, a pervasive problem among students with ADHD.

Teacher: Let's do some long division problems together. Before we get started, can someone tell me what rule everyone should follow during this time? *(sets rule with student input)*

Bill: You have to raise your hand to talk.

Teacher: That's right. The hand-raising rule is in effect. Okay, here's the problem: What is 968 divided by 4? *(teacher writes the problem on the board)* What's the first step? *(involves student)*

Lisa: 242 *(She calls out the correct answer without raising her hand. Teacher scans the classroom and notices that two other students have raised their hands and remained silent.)*

Teacher: Lisa, that's an interruption. *(prudent corrective feedback)* I liked the way Miguel and Susan remembered to raise their hands. *(strategic praise)* Miguel, what's the first step? *(involves student)*

In this example, the teacher correctly enforced the hand-raising rule while teaching. This usually takes active attention to the class process. It is often tempting to respond to the student who calls out, especially if the answer is correct, and accept it. However, this means that the hand-raising rule is not enforced. In effect, the students who follow this rule end up being punished and the students who violate the rule are reinforced. The result is that students learn not to take the class rules seriously. Remember, students with

ADHD may be particularly susceptible to this negative learning process. Here again, your role as a teacher involves not only teaching academic concepts but also teaching students how to follow rules and directions.

GUIDELINES FOR SCANNING THE CLASS TO PROMOTE GOOD ATTENTION AND BEHAVIOR

Develop the habit of thinking about the lesson plan and behavior simultaneously, weaving smoothly from teaching to managing attention and behavior and back to teaching. As illustrated above, management for behavior should be brief (a few seconds). Emphasize positive behaviors ("I see Cornell working." "I like the way Sherri is listening." "Looks like the entire first row is paying attention.") and involve students in the lesson ("Tasha, tell me what punctuation mark goes at the end of this sentence." "Mark, what is the answer to this math problem?") Other strategies, such as setting rules and giving clear directions ("Everyone, get your math book and open to page 25."), should be used to promote compliance and prevent problem behavior. Corrective feedback ("That's an interruption." "That's minus one point for not following directions.") should be used to stop disruptive behavior.

The timing of strategies is critical since you want to catch good behavior before it stops and stop negative behavior before it gets out of hand. On average, set your mental clock for about one or two minutes. Scan your classroom at this interval looking for a student (especially the ADHD student) who is attending or on task and involve the student or give positive attention. During your scan, you should also keep your eyes open for students who are inattentive or silently daydreaming. Involve or redirect them. Students who are being disruptive should receive immediate corrective feedback. If behavior is mostly positive, you will probably need to praise a couple of times per scan. If behavior is very problematic, you may need to take more time during your scan so that you can provide feedback to more students. During each scan, you should try to give positive attention and/or involve a student (or students) in the lesson. Remember that asking students questions or having them participate in the lesson in some way is a great way to help them maintain attention to the task.

If you teach a lower grade or have many behavior problems in your class, you may need to scan the class more frequently than the one- to two-minute guideline so that you can be sure to catch good behavior when it happens. On the other hand, if you have few behavior problems or you teach a higher grade, you should be able to lengthen this interval. Likewise, you should vary this approach for different activities and class periods. During high

> **DURING YOUR SCAN, YOU SHOULD ALSO KEEP YOUR EYES OPEN FOR STUDENTS WHO ARE INATTENTIVE OR SILENTLY DAYDREAMING. INVOLVE OR REDIRECT THEM.**
>
> ■ ■ ■

interest or hands-on activities, frequent management of behavior may be unnecessary to maintain attention to task. During times when students with ADHD are prone to having difficulty staying on task, such as during independent seatwork, lengthy lessons, or transitions, frequent involvement and feedback may be critical. Keep in mind that when most of the class is working during independent seatwork, it is better to move close to the off-task student and give a brief redirection in a low tone of voice.

When you are first learning this approach, you may find it hard to scan every one or two minutes. You might be more successful if you start with less frequent scans until you get the hang of it. You should also plan and practice using these strategies. Before or after class, plan what behavior you want to attend to, how you can involve students, and what directions and corrective statements you may need to make. Then, practice doing it. With planning and practice, these sorts of methods should become much easier, even automatic. Chapter 4 describes how to add more potent interventions to these basic methods.

CHAPTER 4

INDIVIDUALIZED BEHAVIOR PROGRAMS: WHEN MORE IS NEEDED

Until now, we have discussed basic interventions useful for the entire classroom. These interventions are part of what's considered good classroom management. Most students respond to these basic strategies, but students with ADHD often need more. This section is specifically designed for those cases needing more potent interventions. These interventions can be administered by a single teacher, but in some cases, they can better be undertaken by a classroom aide trained in behavioral interventions.

ASSESSING BEHAVIOR

The first thing you will need to do is specify very clearly what the problem is and what may be triggering and maintaining it. Why is this so important? The reason is based on the fact that students with ADHD are quite diverse in terms of the problems they exhibit, the cause of their problems, and their response to different behavioral interventions. We need to know the specific problems a child exhibits before we can design effective behavior change programs.

DEFINING THE BEHAVIOR OF CONCERN

Problems may arise due to too much inappropriate behavior (e.g., interrupting) or too little appropriate behavior (e.g., not completing enough work). Be very specific and clear about the problem. Translate global personality traits into observable, specific behaviors. For example, laziness might be defined as "not completing assigned work"; bossiness might be defined as "name-calling" or "making demands of others"; and forgetfulness might be defined as "failing to turn in completed homework." Why is it important to be so specific? Behaviors are easier to change than personality traits. Behaviors are easier for people to agree on. Behaviors are also more objective and less susceptible to bias.

Once you have identified the problem you are concerned about, you are ready to identify what may be triggering and maintaining it. Identify what happens right before the problem occurs. These are things that may have precipitated or set off the problem. Ask yourself whether the problem behavior generally occurs:

1. At the same time of day (beginning or end of the day, during transitions)?

2. While a specific subject is being taught?

3. When a certain task is given (writing, listening, sit quietly)?

4. When a particular instruction format is in effect: large-group lesson, individual seatwork, center-focused activities, cooperative learning activity, and so on?

5. When the student is around certain peers?

6. In response to a classmate's teasing or provocation?

7. In response to a direction from you (to get started, to finish quickly, to do something s/he does not want to do)?

8. At recess or other less structured times of the day?

9. When the student is overstimulated or excited?

10. When the student perceives an assignment or task as boring, too difficult, or one s/he does not understand?

Identify what happens right after the problem behavior occurs. These are things that can maintain the problem. When the problem behavior occurs or the desired behavior fails to occur, ask yourself whether the student:

1. Gets out of doing any work?

2. Gets attention from peers (be it positive or negative)?

3. Gets his or her way?

4. Gets someone to do an undesirable/difficult task for him or her?

5. Sees you get frustrated or angry (this can be a reinforcer)?

6. Disrupts the class?

7. Gets positive attention from you? (For example, some teachers try to discourage off-task behavior with comments such as "I know you can behave better. Is something wrong?" This kind of response can reinforce the problem.)

MONITORING BEHAVIORS AND KEEPING RECORDS

The best way to find out what sets off or maintains problems in a given situation is to keep a written record, like the one below, of what was going on several days prior to and following the problem behavior.

DAY	PROBLEM BEHAVIOR	WHAT WAS HAPPENING WHEN IT OCCURRED?	WHAT HAPPENED JUST AFTER IT OCCURRED?
Monday	Andy tipped his chair over and fell.	Students were taking turns reading sections of their history books and following along.	The students near Andy laughed. I told Andy that it wouldn't have happened if he had been sitting properly. He seemed to enjoy the attention. I became angry.

After you have tracked the behavior for a few days, you can look for patterns (Does it always seem to happen at the same time? Is the child usually successful in getting the attention of his peers or a negative, emotional reaction from you?). Based on what seems to trigger or maintain the problem, you can decide on interventions. For example, if the problem behavior is always followed by the same thing (such as, the student ends up getting out of doing some of his work), the most effective intervention may be to change the consequence of the negative behavior (make sure the student has to complete all assigned work before earning basic privileges such as recess). Likewise, if the problem is always set off by the same thing (e.g., a difficult task), the most effective intervention may be to modify that which sets it off (break the task down into smaller parts that are easier to understand). If the problem seems to occur because the student is trying to avoid doing certain tasks, you might try changing the task in a way to make it more enjoyable or have the student earn a privilege for completing the task. Sometimes it is hard to know exactly what is causing any given problem. If you don't see any particular patterns, don't give up! There are many strategies that work even when you are not sure of the exact cause of the problem.

It is usually a good idea to find out how often or for how long the problem occurs before you start a behavior change program. This is called getting a baseline of the behavior. Getting a baseline may take some time, but it is important to be as objective as you can in observing the behavior. It is all too easy to overestimate the frequency of a problem when it is highly disruptive or particularly annoying to us. We also tend to overestimate problems as a function of our own moods, levels of stress, and so on. Similarly, we can also underestimate the frequency of a problem. We may be especially vulnerable to this when the behavior is not very disruptive (e.g., daydreaming). Knowing how often or for how long the problem behavior occurs before you start an intervention will also help you set fair and realistic goals for the student.

To find out how often a behavior occurs you can simply keep a tally.

BEHAVIOR	9:00-10:30	10:30-12:00	12:00-2:00
Interruptions			
Raised hand			

To find out how long a behavior lasts, record its duration.

LENGTH OF SUCCESSIVE OCCURRENCES OF BEHAVIOR					
BEHAVIOR	1	2	3	4	5
Out of seat	15 minutes	5 minutes			
Worked on assignment	10 minutes out of 30 minutes				

SELECTING TARGET BEHAVIORS AND GOALS

Once you have defined the problem, you are ready to select specific target behaviors. Target behaviors are those behaviors you would like the student to be doing instead of the problem behavior. For example, if the problem is being disruptive during independent seatwork, the target behavior might be completing work quietly. If the problem is fighting, the target behavior might be getting along with others. Here are some popular target behaviors for students with ADHD.

- ⮌ Follows directions: follows directions given by teacher within reasonable period of time (or with X or fewer reminders)

- ⮌ Follows class rules: sits properly and remains seated unless given permission to leave seat; talks only when given permission by teacher

- ⮌ Completes class work: does work accurately and neatly

- ⮌ Works quietly: no talking or noise-making without teacher permission

- ⮌ Keeps desk clean: desk area is organized and clean at specified check points

- ⮌ Completes homework: completes and turns in homework with acceptable accuracy and neatness

- ⮌ Gets along with peers: gets along with peers without teasing or fighting; cooperates and shares

- ⮌ Gets started right away: starts work or assigned activity within time specified by teacher or with X or fewer reminders

- ⮌ Stays on task while working

- ⮌ Asks for help when it's needed

- ⮌ Follows recess rules: obeys staff, cleans up, lines up, is not benched

GUIDELINES FOR SELECTING TARGET BEHAVIORS AND GOALS

1. Start out simple. Have only one target behavior. However, if you use a token economy (see page 86), you may want to start with three or four target behaviors.

2. If the most important target behavior from your standpoint will be a difficult goal for the child, avoid the temptation to tackle that one first. It is important to start out successfully, so make sure these first behavioral goals are easy to achieve. You may start out implementing the program during the morning hours and then add the afternoon hours once the child shows improvement in the morning.

3. It is usually better to reward a positive behavior than to reward the absence of a negative behavior. Otherwise, you run the risk of not teaching the student a better alternative. For example, if the problem is calling out, it is better to reward hand-raising (the positive behavior), than the absence of calling out (the problem behavior). If you only reward not calling out, you may inadvertently reinforce the student for not participating at all. Notice how each of the target behaviors listed earlier is worded as a behavior to increase.

4. Whenever academic productivity is a problem, make sure to select an academic target behavior such as completing assignments or turning in complete homework. Don't just simply reward the student for staying on task. If you do, work productivity may not increase. An additional benefit of rewarding academic performance is that it often improves behavior at the same time.

5. Involve students in setting their goals. Fran Martin of Paddock Lane School, Beatrice, Nebraska, finds it important to set goals *with* students, not *for* students. She explains that problems are like "roadblocks." She asks students what their roadblocks are (e.g., talking too much in class) and what ways they can think of to help themselves. She has kids complete their own goal sheets where they decide what they want to achieve. The more involved the students are in setting goals the more likely they are to achieve them.

6. Set the goal for the target behavior at a realistic level of performance—that is, a level at which you think the student can succeed. Gather baseline data to find out what the level is, observing how often the student achieves the goal without your doing anything. For example, how long can the student work quietly? How many assignments does the student currently complete? How often is the student interrupting? How often is the student aggressive? Once you have an idea of this baseline of behavior, you can set a small, reasonable goal for the student. Some teachers plan to set the goal at no more than 20 percent better than the student is already doing. For example, if a student is not completing any work, set the goal at completing 20 percent of assigned work, rather than all of the work. If a student is interrupting

15 times a day, set the goal at no more than 10 interruptions. As the student shows improvement, the goal can and should be increased. But remember to focus on improvement, not perfection!

MOTIVATING BEHAVIOR CHANGE

Once you've selected a target behavior and set the goals, the next step is to establish incentives to motivate behavior change. We discussed the importance of positive attention and how to use your attention strategically to encourage appropriate behavior. Although positive attention can go far, it often does not go far enough for students with ADHD. Remember that students with ADHD have motivational systems, most likely biologically based, which usually require more tangible, concrete rewards to inhibit their impulses and focus on the task at hand (Pfiffner et al., 2006). This often means using activities, privileges, and/or token economies as rewards.

USING ACTIVITIES AND PRIVILEGES AS REWARDS

Activities and privileges that children enjoy are usually included as part of the normal routine in most classrooms. They can also be used as rewards to teach students good behavior and work habits. When used as rewards, certain activities and/or privileges are given only after a student meets a specific goal. For this to be effective, you must identify rewards that are meaningful to the student. There are several ways to do this.

- Consider what the student likes or asks to do.

- Observe what the child does when given free time. The things the child chooses to do are likely to be good rewards.

- Ask the student what he or she likes to do; ask what he or she would like to work for or earn. Use the sample survey on page 84 as a model.

- Take advantage of what's referred to as the Premack principle. This principle states that a low-probability activity (one that doesn't happen very often) can be increased by following it with a high-probability activity (one that happens a lot). For example, one teacher found that completing assignments was a very low-probability behavior for one of her students. On the other hand, a high-probability behavior for this student was drawing pictures. The student would spend all day drawing if it was left up to him. This teacher decided to use drawing time as a reward. For each assignment completed, the student earned a brief period of time for drawing.

⮑ If you can, use activities that double as good learning experiences. David Agler calls these "2 for 1's." For example, he incorporates money lessons into a weekly movie theater reinforcer where kids watch a movie on a school TV. Kids use their points to buy movie tickets and snack bar items.

In the box below is a sample survey you can use to find out what activities and privileges a student likes.

KARA'S FAVORITE THINGS AT SCHOOL

What classroom activities do you like best?
free reading and stamp club

What privileges do you like to have at school?
being line leader

What is a good prize your teacher could give you?
cool pencils and erasers; stickers

What are your favorite food treats that you can have at school?
popcorn

What do you like to do most during free time at school?
play card games

Who do you like to spend your time with at school?
my friends

What would you like to do more often at school?
read books of my choice

Below is a list of activities, privileges, and tangible rewards that many teachers have found to be effective motivators for students with ADHD.

SUGGESTED SCHOOL REWARDS	
Art/craft project	Librarian for the day
Baseball cards	Lining up first
Being the class monitor	Watching DVD/ listening to music
Being teacher's helper	Lotteries/raffles
Bringing in something from home	Lunch with a friend
Certificates/awards	Lunch with the teacher or principal
Choice time for activities	Making something for bulletin board
Choosing where to sit in class	Movies in class
Colorful pencils	Picking another student with whom to do something
Cooking activity	Removing the lowest grade or making up a missing grade
Eating lunch in special area	Running errands
Erasing whiteboards	Sitting in special area of class (bean bag chairs)
Extra computer time	Snacks or other food treats
Extra "free" time	Stamps
Extra recess or extra lunch	Stickers
Field trips	Stuffed animal to adopt for the night
Free reading or being read to	Taking care of class animals
Free time with friend	Treasure chest
Fun erasers	Treasure hunt
Game of hangman	Writing on whiteboard
Game of kids against teacher	
Games in class	
Good note home to parents	
Grab bag with small toys or school supplies	
Having a classwork or homework pass	
Helping correct papers	

SETTING UP AN ACTIVITY-BASED REWARD PROGRAM

Below is a worksheet to help you design an individual program using activities and privileges as rewards. Note that students with ADHD need immediate rewards. Have them earn the activity or privilege on a daily basis for the most positive result. Here is a sample program developed by a teacher to address a student's disruptive behavior during math period.

---

1. What is the behavior I'm concerned about? Be specific. _noise making_

2. How often does it happen? (the baseline) _several times each math period_

3. What do I want the student to be doing instead? (the target behavior)
working and being quiet

4. How many times or for how long must the student do the target behavior to earn a reward? _Kevin has to be quiet and do his work for most of the math period. He can have two reminders and still earn the reward._

5. What activity or privilege can be used as a reward? (Get input from the student.
reduction in math homework

6. When will the reward be given? (Remember, immediate feedback is most effective.)
Kevin will get a homework pass right after math period.

USING TOKEN ECONOMIES

Token economies are another way to teach positive behaviors. In a token economy, students earn tokens such as points, stars, or tickets throughout the day and then later exchange their earnings for what are called "back-up" rewards. The back-up rewards are usually privileges, activities, or tangibles like those listed earlier. Tokens are especially effective for students with ADHD because they can be given right away and often. The back-up rewards can be interesting and varied, and the token bridges the gap between the student's good behavior and the reward. Also, you can use tokens for several different target behaviors. Follow these steps for setting up a token economy.

1. Identify one to four target behaviors you want to change.

2. Select the kind of token to use. Younger children often enjoy tangible tokens such as poker chips, stamps, or color cards. Older children do well with points.

3. Establish times each day for giving the student feedback about the number of tokens earned. This is usually several times a day (e.g., before recess, before lunch, before dismissal, and recess target behaviors directly after recess). For high rates of problems or younger children you may want to provide feedback as often as every half hour. Do not wait until the end of the day to give feedback; for best effect, provide feedback at least several times during the day.

4. Decide on back-up rewards that tokens can buy. Use a range of privileges and activities listed in the form of a "reward menu" to make sure there is enough variety and novelty. Remember that what is reinforcing to one child may not be reinforcing to another. Also, only use rewards that can be withheld if not earned. For example, if activities such as art, sports, or free time cannot be withheld, don't use them as rewards.

5. Operationalize the target behavior. The behaviors need to be clearly laid out so that the student knows exactly what is required to earn the tokens for the target behavior (e.g., following rules with no more than three reminders). Describe and demonstrate what it means to be exhibiting the target behavior versus not exhibiting it (i.e., following the rules versus not following the rules).

6. Set the token value for each behavior. Target behaviors can be weighted according to difficulty level. Those that are easy for the child to accomplish can be worth fewer points.

7. Set the purchase price for rewards. The purchase price for the rewards should be set at a level that doesn't exceed the child's spending power. Don't make it necessary for a child to earn all possible tokens to get a reward. Instead, have rewards available for improvement. The child should be able to be successful right away so that he or she feels confident and stays interested in the program. Usually this means not requiring children to do more than 20 percent better than they are already doing.

8. Give both the opportunity to earn a daily reward based on that day's point total (e.g., extra computer time) and a longer-term reward such as a prize based on the week's total (e.g., free time with a friend, grab bag). Weekly rewards can be based on the number of good days during the week or the total number of tokens earned.

9. Use a form like the one below to keep track of tokens earned each day.

CLASSROOM CHALLENGE

Student: _____ Day: _____

2 = Very good

1 = OK

0 = Needs improvement

Times Assessed	Behavior 1	Behavior 2	Behavior 3
before RECESS	0 1 2	0 1 2	0 1 2
before LUNCH	0 1 2	0 1 2	0 1 2
before DISMISSAL	0 1 2	0 1 2	0 1 2

Total points earned: _____

Signatures: _____   _____

                    Teacher   Student

Rewards:

Comments:

As shown, the chart should include the day of the week, space to list the target behaviors, and space to record the number of tokens (points, in this case) earned. There should be also space to list rewards that points can buy. All parties involved can sign the form to make it an official contract.

Let's look at how a teacher might set up a token economy and review it with a student.

Teacher: Michael, there are some areas at school in which I think you could do better, and I'd like to go over a program I think might help you (*pulls out Classroom Challenge and reads the contents as the student looks on*). These are the areas that I think you could do better in:

➲ Following directions—which means doing what I ask right away

➲ Completing assignments—which means doing all of the assigned work by the time you are supposed to

➲ Raising your hand—which means raising your hand when you have something to say instead of blurting it out

I've set it up so you can get up to two points for each of these three areas three times a day—before recess, before lunch, and before dismissal. To earn a 2 in any area, you would need to have zero or one reminder; for a 1, only two or three reminders; and if you needed more than three reminders, you would earn a 0. We'll record your points on this form. So how many points can you earn each day?

Michael: I can earn six points three times a day, so that comes to 18 points that I can earn a day.

Teacher: That's right! What's your favorite privilege that you would like to work for if you get 17 or 18 points?

Michael: Free reading on the bean bag chair.

Teacher: Okay, that sounds good. You can earn the free reading during our study hall period. How about if you earn 14, 15, or 16 points? That's still a pretty good day overall.

Michael: Computer lab.

Teacher: That's fine. If you get less than 14 points, that means that you had a lot of problems that day. So you wouldn't earn any special privileges. You would just have regular study hall at your desk. To make sure I know you understand, tell me how this program works.

Michael: First I have to work on following directions, completing my work, and raising my hand without reminders. If I get zero or one reminder that's a 2; if I get two or three reminders that's a 1; if I get more than three, that's a 0. We'll check the chart before recess, before lunch, and before dismissal. If I get 17 or 18 points, I get free reading. If I get 14, 15, or 16 points, I get computer lab. Otherwise, I have regular study hall.

Teacher: I think you have it. How do you think you will do?

Michael: Good. I think I can get all 18 points.

Teacher: Great, let's start on Monday.

Michael starts the program on the next school day. He brings the card to his teacher for signature at the end of the three rating periods. (See the card at right.) Here is what the teacher says to him at the end of the last rating period.

Teacher: You earned 2 points for following directions, and 2 points for completing your work, but you forgot to raise your hand several times, so you won't get a point for raising your hand. Let's count your points.

Michael: It comes to 16 points. Computer lab!

Teacher: That's right. What's the one area you need to improve tomorrow?

Michael: Raising my hand.

Teacher: That's right. You did well for the first day; keep up the good work! You can go to computer lab now.

CLASSROOM CHALLENGE

Student: **Michael**   Day: **Monday**

2 = Very good

1 = OK

0 = Needs improvement

Times Assessed	Behavior 1 following directions	Behavior 2 completing assignments	Behavior 3 raising hand
before RECESS	0 1 **(2)**	0 1 **(2)**	0 1 **(2)**
before LUNCH	0 1 **(2)**	0 1 **(2)**	0 1 **(2)**
before DISMISSAL	0 1 **(2)**	0 1 **(2)**	**(0)** 1 2

Total points earned: **16**

Signatures: **Mrs. Smith**   **Michael**
                  Teacher   Student

Rewards: **17 or 18 points = free reading on bean bag chair. 14–16 points = computer lab. Less than 14 points = study hall.**

Comments:
Great Start!

Sample Classroom Challenge

KEYS TO SUCCESS WHEN IMPLEMENTING A TOKEN PROGRAM

1. Be consistent. Don't forget about the program, adhere to the criteria set for tokens, and don't give in.

2. When tokens are earned, provide praise, be enthusiastic, and be sure to follow through, for example: "You did a great job following all the rules today!" Don't say to a student that a token or back-up reward was earned and then later refuse to give the reward because you are upset about another unrelated problem that comes up.

3. When tokens are not earned or are lost, don't lecture or argue with the student. Be matter of fact and brief. You may want to ask the student what he or she needs to work on to earn tokens the next day, for example: "You didn't get your math assignment done today so you don't earn any points. What do you think you can do tomorrow to do better?"

4. Use both daily and longer-term (e.g., weekly, biweekly) rewards. If rewards are only earned once per week (or less), many students with ADHD will lose interest in the program.

5. It is almost always better to use smaller rewards frequently rather than large rewards infrequently.

INDIVIDUAL AND CLASSWIDE REWARD PROGRAMS

Reward programs can be set up for individual students, for groups of students, or for the entire class. Individual programs or classwide programs wherein students earn rewards for their own behavior are usually best for the student with ADHD. Many teachers prefer doing classwide programs since they have found that rewards improve the performance of all children and are easier to use if used for all. Other teachers like to concentrate their efforts on individual children. In either case, designing these programs is part science and part art. Be creative and imaginative; the more enthusiastic you are, the more motivated the students will be. Here are some examples of individual and classwide activity/privilege programs.

Challenge games: In these games, students compete with teachers for tokens during a designated time period. Tokens might be chips, pegs, points, and so on. Students earn tokens by following rules; teachers receive tokens when the student does not follow the rules. Whoever has the most tokens after the time period is up selects an activity for the class. The time period can be increased as students are successful.

Stamps (or stickers): Let students earn stamps when they are working. Use stamps that are fun for kids, like a picture of a bee for those who are working "as busy as a bee." Walk around the class during independent work time and stamp the work of students who are working hard. Use a different stamp for each period/subject, which increases the value of each stamp. For an added twist, you can have each stamp be worth a ticket in a lottery at the end of the week.

On-task thermometer: This is a variation of the Goodsport Thermometer discussed earlier (see page 56). Here, a picture of a thermometer is placed on the student's desk. When the student is on task, the temperature reading is raised. When the student is off task, it's lowered. For periods of time in which the thermometer shows a high temperature, the student earns time doing a special activity of his or her choice at the end of the day (playing a game, drawing with special markers, helping the teacher). If the thermometer becomes so hot (the student is doing so well) that it "breaks," the time is doubled. For periods in which the thermometer is at the lowest point, the student loses minutes of recess or a special activity equal to the time off-task.

Privileges for completed work: Students who complete work with time to spare before the next activity can earn extra free time, free reading, or simple art projects. David Agler has his first- and second-grade students earn time playing a computer game when they finish an assignment. He makes this attractive by having kids preview the "game of the day" ahead of time. You can also use modified homework requirements as a reward. Students can earn the privilege of doing homework during the last 20 minutes of class instead of doing it at home or earn homework passes that they can turn in on one day of their choosing. On that day, students are excused from their homework assignment.

Classwide token economy programs: In these programs, all students can earn tokens (tickets are commonly used) for a variety of behaviors. These might include following class rules, completing assignments, appropriate behavior during transition or at lunch, doing homework, doing work neatly, working quietly, following directions right away, helping others, and lining up properly. Teachers use methods for remembering to issue the tokens (point reviews at the end of each period, tickets in their pockets). Students can keep track of their earnings by entering points on cards or keeping tickets in small plastic bags at their desk. Tokens can then be exchanged at regular intervals (twice per week, weekly, monthly) for purchases from a prize box, class store, or auction table with items such as stickers, tattoos, trading cards, crayons, pencils, and erasers or privileges such as homework passes, line leader designations, or extra free reading certificates. In a variation of this, Suzanne Vighetti uses "good behavior" tickets as an incentive for her kindergarten students at Franklin Elementary School in Bethel Park, Pennsylvania. Children earn tickets for things such as putting their name on their papers, sitting up straight and listening, and coloring neatly. They write their name on tickets they earn and put them in a class jar. Vighetti draws tickets from the jar randomly during the day. Children whose tickets are drawn earn rewards such as being first in line or getting the mail or a prize from the prize box (pencils, erasers, trinkets, seasonal things). She adds an element of surprise to the program by "sneaking up" behind students and giving them tickets privately while they are working. Vighetti also sometimes staples a ticket onto a student's good work. She varies how she uses the ticket system depending upon the needs of her class but usually has ticket drawings every day (and sometimes several times a day), especially at the beginning, to keep her young students motivated.

Kid bucks with an auction: Jay Teeman uses a kid-bucks system in his fifth-grade class at Roscomare Road Elementary School in Los Angeles, California. All 33 students earn dollars every day for being responsible and well behaved, showing good academic skills, working together, and reaching individual goals in areas of need. They also earn dollars for completing projects and getting good grades. Additionally, students can get paid for doing a variety of jobs in class such as being a teacher's helper, cleaning up the class library, being an office monitor, passing out items, and helping someone on the computer. Students can lose dollars for talking, not turning in homework, and not taking their turn as play leader. Students spend their dollars at class auctions. They can buy things such as stickers, candy, baseball cards, posters, and comics.

Token economy using a checkbook: Andrea Hauber uses a token economy with her fifth-graders at Casey Middle School in Williamsville, New York. She has five rules posted in the classroom: be respectful, obey adults, stay on task, work quietly, and raise hand/wait to be called on.

Students earn points throughout the day for a wide variety of behaviors such as answering questions correctly when called on, answering attention checks correctly, turning in completed homework, getting started right away, moving quickly and quietly during transitions, and having an organized backpack and locker during checks. Students lose points for behaviors such as violations of the five rules, not answering attention checks correctly, and not having an organized locker or backpack. Students can also earn bonus points for "perfect days" (i.e., no point losses). Each student receives a "checkbook" (which they decorate) to keep track of their point earnings and losses. They can spend their checkbook points for a variety of rewards at the end of the day or week varying from inexpensive items such as fun erasers, pencils, stickers, Jolly Ranchers, and M&Ms to more expensive items (earned weekly or monthly) such as homework passes. High-point earners for the week get to use the rolling, comfy chair on Fridays. Students are eligible to spend their points if they have the requisite number and also as long as they have no more than the maximum allowable losses. Point requirements are increased as students are successful throughout the school year in continually improving their behavior. Hauber reports that her students love this system and that she finds it easy to use because the rules are consistent and the system has become part of her routine.

Intensive token economy in a small-class setting: A schoolwide token program designed specifically to meet the needs of students with ADHD is in effect at the UCI-CDC school (which exclusively serves students with ADHD). Each class has a maximum of 15 students, taught by one teacher and one aide, and the school day is divided into 30-minute periods. Students earn a maximum of 20 points each period for the following behaviors: getting started on their work, following directions and class rules, staying on task, getting along with peers, and cleaning up. During each period, students are told when they are earning or not earning points. At the end of each period is a "point check" during which students are told how many points they have earned or what color "patrol" they have earned. Color patrols correspond to points earned as follows: Red patrol equals 90 percent or more of possible points earned; yellow patrol equals 80–89 percent of possible points earned; blue patrol equals below 80 percent of possible points earned. Points and percentages are emphasized with the older students; colors are emphasized with the younger students. Students' earnings are posted on a board displayed in class. In grades 2–6, students report how well they think they did. If their self-rating matches the teacher's rating, they earn bonus points. During the last 20 minutes of the day, students earn reinforcement based on their earnings that day. The higher their earnings, the greater the number of choices they have for reinforcement. Students earning red patrol, or 90 percent or more of possible points, have the most choices. They can choose from all centers and reinforcement activities such as computer time, "red patrol" games, art supplies (the favorite ones), outside play, or any of the activities listed for the other levels of reward. Students earning yellow patrol, or 80–89 percent of points possible, earn fewer choices, which include watching (but not playing) any red patrol activity, "yellow patrol" games, art supplies (less favorite ones), card games, and puzzles. Students earning blue patrol, or less than 80 percent of points possible, have the fewest choices. They stay at their seats and read or write with pencils and paper.

Students also earn weekly rewards based on the week's total. Weekly rewards might be movies, taco or pizza fests, water play, special games, special art projects, or field trips. Students also progress through a levels system based on their ability to maintain positive behavior (i.e., red patrol behavior) over an extended period of time. Increased privileges are provided for maintaining responsible and appropriate behavior and moving up the levels. All students start at Level 1, where they receive the fewest basic privileges and the most feedback. At this level they are allowed to bring a book to school. After one to two weeks of red patrol and correct matches (older students only), they move to Level 2, which includes increased privileges such as lining up second, increased choices of where to eat at lunch, and access to "Level 2 chairs" (ones in a more desirable location). After another couple of weeks of earning red patrol, they advance to Level 3. At Level 3, the frequency of feedback is reduced and students earn privileges such as lining up first, sitting in "Level 3 chairs" (ones in the most desirable locations), eating in area of choice, and being a teacher's helper. Students at this level also can bring something to school to share during the weekly class sharing time. At higher levels, they earn the opportunity to be the teacher's assistant in handing out materials, using the copy machine, helping the teacher dismiss kids (or line up), and other privileges such as greater access to water and the bathroom; at Level 10, they can earn a cookie party/play time and can invite someone at a lower level to attend the party if they choose. Students can also move through a challenge level and a transition level, which serves as a way to gradually "fade out" the program (see Fading Reward Programs, page 108)

This more intensive program is most needed when working with students who have severe ADHD symptoms. Having a small class size and, in some cases, having a behavioral aide assist with implementation helps make the programs work. However, teachers of general education classes with up to

> INCREASED PRIVILEGES ARE PROVIDED FOR MAINTAINING RESPONSIBLE AND APPROPRIATE BEHAVIOR AND MOVING UP THE LEVELS. ALL STUDENTS START AT LEVEL I, WHERE THEY RECEIVE THE FEWEST BASIC PRIVILEGES AND THE MOST FEEDBACK.
>
> ■ ■ ■

30 students (but only a few having ADHD) have implemented modified versions of this program with success.

Using classroom aides to implement a token economy in the general education classroom: For students who require very frequent monitoring and feedback, a classroom aide may be necessary to assist the teacher in implementing the token economy in a regular classroom. The Irvine Paraprofessional Program provides a model for this approach in the general education classroom (Kotkin, 1995). Paraprofessionals, with extensive training in behavioral interventions, serve as classroom aides to assist with the implementation of the token economy. The paraprofessionals implement the token economy with identified students during morning hours. The teacher operates the token economy in the afternoon. The child receives tokens (stamps) for up to four target behaviors during designated time periods as indicated on the sample form on page 97. When the paraprofessionals are in the class, the time period is every 15 minutes. In the afternoon, when the teacher is implementing the program, the time periods are longer (45 minutes) to make the program more practical for the teacher to do. In addition to the feedback at the end of each period, students are given one to three reminders during each period to do the target behavior.

At the end of the day, students bring their daily report cards to a school-based reinforcement center where the stamps they have earned on the card are exchanged for a choice of a 20-minute activity. The more points earned, the greater the choice of activities (computer games are popular). A sample daily report card is on the next page.

The program also includes a three-tier levels system where students earn privileges as they move up each of three levels by consistently reaching daily and weekly goals. The levels system also provides a mechanism to fade the program since feedback intervals are increased (from 15 minutes to one hour) and the frequency of reminders are reduced as students achieve higher levels. The goal is to fade the program to a level in which the teacher can take over without assistance from the paraprofessional and still maintain the students' positive behavior.

JASON'S CLASSROOM CHALLENGE

MORNING SCHEDULE 8:00–12:00

On-Task Behavior

Staying Seated: Receive one stamp every 15 minutes that you remain seated. Getting out of seat with teacher's permission is OK.

8:15   8:30   8:45   9:00   9:15   9:30   Snack
10:15   10:30   10:45   11:00   11:30   11:45

Working Quietly: Receive one stamp every 15 minutes if you do not visit with your neighbor or make distracting noises or gestures. Visiting neighbor with the teacher's permission is OK.

8:15   8:30   8:45   9:00   9:15   9:30   Snack
10:15   10:30   10:45   11:00   11:30   11:45

Academic Performance

Amount of Work Completed: Receive one stamp every 15 minutes if you complete assigned work during that period. During class discussions, stamps will be awarded if you are paying attention to the activity.

8:15   8:30   8:45   9:00   9:15   9:30   Snack
10:15   10:30   10:45   11:00   11:30   11:45

Accuracy of Work: If 90 percent or more of your work is completed accurately and it is neat, you will receive one stamp every 15 minutes. During class discussions, stamps will be awarded if your contributions are accurate or task related.

8:15   8:30   8:45   9:00   9:15   9:30   Snack
10:15   10:30   10:45   11:00   11:30   11:45

AFTERNOON SCHEDULE 12:45–2:00

Staying Seated: Earn 4 stamps every half hour that you remain seated.

1:15   1:45

Working Quietly: Receive 4 stamps every half hour if you do not visit with your neighbor or make distracting noises.

1:15   1:45

Amount of Work Completed: If you complete all work assigned, you will receive 4 stamps every half hour.

1:15   1:45

Accuracy of Work: If 90% or more of work is completed accurately and is neat, you will receive 4 stamps every half hour.

1:15   1:45

Total stamps possible = 80   Total stamps earned: _____

Reward

72 or more stamps = 90%   Computer games
64 to 71 stamps = 80%   Free reading
66 to 70 stamps = 70%   Study hall

GROUP AND TEAM REWARD PROGRAMS

So far, we've talked mostly about rewards that children can earn for themselves. You can also set up group reward programs where each student works toward earning a reward that his or her group or the whole class shares. Many teachers find these programs more practical to use in large classrooms than individual token economies since the token recording system is less cumbersome and fewer rewards are needed. When working toward a group reward, kids often encourage one another to be well behaved and are more inclined to ignore their classmates' negative behavior. After all, the better their classmates do, the sooner they earn the reward. If you do use group reward programs, though, expect that students with ADHD may also need rewards that are directly tied to their own behavior and not dependent on the class. Also be careful: Some kids may try to sabotage the program by purposely exhibiting negative behavior. Make sure that no single child can have this kind of control over the whole class.

When you first use a group reward, set it up so that students can earn the reward fairly quickly (e.g., within a week). When they see how fun and rewarding it is, you can increase the time and requirements for earning the next group reward. Never have group rewards take longer than a month to earn or students may lose interest. You should also have a way of depicting students' progress toward earning the reward. Some teachers use marbles in a jar; others post pictures and diagrams related to the reward on the wall.

Visually tracking progress toward specific activity/privilege reward.

A popular approach is to have the class work toward a pre-identified class reward such as a party or movie. Some teachers use tokens such as marbles in a jar or kernels of corn to track progress. When the jar is full, the reward is earned (in the case of the corn kernels, these could be popped at a popcorn party). Another approach is to make a poster with a picture of the reward and a way to track their daily progress toward earning the reward. Students would earn the reward after they earn enough tokens to reach the reward. Here are some examples.

Gumballs for lining up: David Agler has clear rules for a good lineup, which include keeping hands and feet to oneself. For each lineup where the students follow all of the rules, they earn a gumball sticker on a picture of a gumball jar posted on the wall chart in class. When all empty gumballs have stickers, the class earns the privilege of chewing gum for 30 minutes during reading time. Agler modifies this for even more fun impact, for example, he uses green gumballs for St Patrick's Day and some gumballs are labeled as automatic winners (where kids earn the chewing gum privilege at the next reading period)!

Parties: Theme parties are usually popular rewards. Progress toward earning a party with a food theme can be depicted with a picture of the food item to be earned (pizza, nachos, cookie) posted on a wall in the classroom. Students earn stickers (of pepperonis, chips, and so on), which can be affixed to the picture of the food item, and when full (e.g., pizza full of pepperonis, plate full of chips, cookie full of chocolate chips) the party is earned. Parties can be brief (20–30 minutes) and are best held either at the end of the day or right before recess. *Suggestion:* Have students' parents send in the food (or ingredients) for the parties.

Treasure chest: Many teachers use trinkets (carnival prizes bought in bulk) in a treasure chest as rewards. One teacher posted a picture of a ship sailing toward a treasure chest on an island. For every 15 minutes that the class was working during independent seatwork, she moved the ship one inch closer to the treasure chest on the island. When the ship reached the treasure chest, the class earned the reward (a trinket from the treasure chest for every student).

Movies: This popular activity can also be made into a group reward. One teacher accomplished this in a creative and interesting way by hanging a poster with a picture of students walking to a theater. The class progressed one inch closer to the theater for every 15 minutes they were working and on task. When the students reached the theater, they earned the movie.

Teams and tournaments.

Students can be divided into teams, and teams compete to see who can earn the most points (tokens) in a day. You can increase the incentive value of the tokens by keeping daily tallies of points (on a poster or whiteboard in the class) as though they were standings in a sporting league. You can also have groups assign themselves unique names. Examples of team rewards are the use of table and row points. Students earn points for their team (table or row) by showing target behaviors specified by the teacher. These might be staying on task, putting work away promptly, following directions, working quietly, writing agendas accurately, completing homework, getting along with others, keeping their area clean, and following class rules. Students from tables or rows with the most points after a specified period of time earn the reward (an item from a classroom store, a 10-minute "party" where kids in winning groups can sit outside and eat peanuts or popcorn). It should not take longer than one or two weeks to earn a reward; as students are successful, this period can be lengthened. *Note:* If all teams achieve a certain goal, all should earn the reward. Also, some teachers like to change the groupings every couple of months so that students have a chance to work with everyone. A simpler approach to competitive group rewards (without tokens) commonly used in classrooms can also be effective (e.g., the table that cleans up first gets to line up first for recess).

Another example of a team approach is the Good Behavior Game (Barrish, Saunders, & Wold, 1969), which has been evaluated in many research studies with very impressive positive effects. In this game, the classroom is placed into teams (children with disruptive behavior problems should be divided equally among the teams). The teacher explains what specific behaviors cannot be displayed while the game is going on. During the game, each time a student exhibits disruptive or aggressive behavior, the teacher gives that student's team a checkmark on the whiteboard. After a specified period of time, both teams earn a reward if their checkmarks do not exceed a certain number; otherwise, the team with the fewest marks wins. Tangible daily rewards are important when starting the game and might include stickers or stamps in a booklet, wearing a victory tag, or writing their name on a "Winner's Chart"; intangible rewards are added as students are successful (e.g., lining up first at lunch, free time at the end of the day). Weekly rewards are added after the first week. Students who do not earn rewards are instructed to do quiet seatwork without special attention from the teacher. The length of time in which this game is in effect starts at 10 minutes per day and is gradually increased over time, so that eventually it covers the entire day and students learn to monitor their own behavior. This is a relatively simple approach with long-term positive effects. Research studies show that students participating in this program in their first- and second-grade classrooms had less disruptive, impulsive, and antisocial behavior and fewer substance abuse problems years later than those not receiving this intervention (see www.evidencebasedprograms. org/static/pdfs/GBG%20Manual.pdf for a complete manual describing this program). *Troubleshooting:* If a few students seem to sabotage the game, have those students form a separate team. It is important to be consistent in assigning points and to avoid verbal arguments.

Schoolwide group rewards. Kathleen Healy, a fifth-grade teacher at M.S. 180 in the Bronx, New York, teaches in a departmentalized school, where there are six fifth-grade classes of approximately 35 students each. Each class of students has five main teachers and classrooms to go to. In order to help all students be successful with multiple teachers and classrooms, a schoolwide group reward is in place. The six classes compete against one another for class rewards. Rewards are earned based on points accumulated by each class. Teachers assign a grade (which is translated to points) to each class at the end of every period based on members' overall behavior and work habits during that period. A "grade leader" for the fifth-grade monitors the children closely and also distributes points during lunch, recess, and at other times when students may need help in remembering to follow the rules (e.g., when a substitute teacher is present). The grade leader keeps track of all of the points earned by each of the six classes. At regular intervals, the classes with the most points earn rewards such as special Friday recess, field trips, parties (pizza and soda parties are awarded four times a year to the class with the most points), treats (candy treats are awarded to classes with the second- and third-highest number of points at the quarterly reward period), and choice of where to sit during school movies. To maximize motivation, even for the more problematic classes, all classes earn a "first place" standing at some time during the year. To make sure this happens, the grade leader may set up special challenges such as the opportunity to earn bonus points during lunch or recess. Children with a pattern of behavior problems are prevented from sabotaging their class's success, since their point losses are not counted against the class. Instead, an individual daily school-home contract is set up for them. This school also has a student of the month program which gives an award to one student per grade each month for "doing the right thing." The award is open to most students as it is not based on excelling in the academic arena.

THE IMPORTANCE OF NOVELTY AND CREATIVITY

Students with ADHD are notorious for losing interest in rewards. Expect and accept this. Probably the best way to deal with this is to change rewards regularly. Plan on having to change some rewards at least every week or two. Using a reward menu (containing a list of potential rewards) and having students pick their own rewards can help increase variety. Changing the "packaging" of a reward is also recommended. This is something like good salesmanship and involves making the reward seem more fun and interesting by virtue of how you present it to the student. Teachers know that novelty and presentation are often more important than cost. In many of the examples given earlier, the packaging was intentionally made to be captivating (e.g., using colorful posters depicting the reward the class was to earn: filling a gumball machine, walking to a theater, sailing to a treasure island). You might also consider using different reward themes corresponding to the time of year or an upcoming holiday. Themes can then be changed every month or so.

The words you use can also invite student interest. Call target social skills doing the "smooth move of the day/week." Tell students they are members of the "Hand-Raisers Club." Call individual reward programs "special challenges" or "bonus rewards." Label special chairs that kids earn to sit in ("King's Chair") or call tokens earned for target skills "Big Deals" (they're a big deal to earn). At the UCI-CDC school, "Big Deal" earnings are posted on a wall chart and when the class earns a predetermined number, they have a fiesta. As a variation on this theme, David Agler uses tokens he calls "Mystery Big Deals." The mystery is that he uses invisible ink to mark the number of points earned on a card (token). The child who earns the Mystery Big Deal scratches off the card to see how many points are earned. You could also write actual activities on the card for the child to scratch off. The child would earn the activity written on the card. Another effective reward used by a teacher involves having students earn clean-up duty. Clean-up duty was turned into a desired privilege by having students don white hats and coats and call themselves the "clean-up crew." The students loved it! (These same kids probably hate cleaning their rooms at home.) And yet another idea: Agler has students earn Honest Abe coupons—for telling the truth. He also conducts the "pocket checks game" or "rabbit ears" when students are having difficulty with "taking" things which do not belong to them. In this game, students open their pockets (pockets outside pants look like rabbit ears) to show they have not brought anything from home or taken anything from another student or the school. The game is conducted as often as deemed necessary and is done in a non-humiliating way. Agler finds that kids like to show off their empty pockets.

To increase novelty, multiple ongoing rewards with creative, fun names can be very motivating. Agler says that he likes to create a carnival atmosphere in his classroom with various rewards, including games of chance, that students can earn for good behavior. For example, students can earn a shopping day at the school mall to spend the school dollars they earned by being on red patrol. They can buy school supplies, creative play things, and small snacks with their dollars at the school store. The store is stocked with auction items donated by parents. A few other reward games developed by Agler include the following:

"Gumball Guess" game: Students earn the chance to guess the color of the gumball Agler picks; if correct they earn a trip to the fishing bucket.

"Fishing Bucket" reward: Students get to dip their magnetic fishing pole into a bucket containing money attached to a paper clip. They can spend the money they get at the school store.

Random/intermittent rewards: The opportunity to play the following games can be earned by students throughout the day or week for specific behaviors:

- **Number cube game:** Dice are rolled and if the student correctly guesses the sum that comes up on the dice, he or she earns a treasure chest dip.

- **Popper game:** A game popper with a dice inside is pressed, and if the student correctly guesses the number, he or she wins a treasure chest dip.

- **Spin spinner:** A spinner with numbers is spun. If the student correctly guesses the number the spinner lands on, he or she wins the treasure chest dip.

With all reward programs, it is important that goals be within reach from the beginning. At first kids should get the chance to earn (e.g., dollars from the fishing bucket) right away or earn treasure chest dips, but once they are successful, rewards can and should be faded to an intermittent schedule.

USING A CONTRACT

You can formalize almost any behavior program by writing a contract between you and the student. Contracts are particularly useful for older students. On the contract you should make it clear what your responsibilities are and what the student's responsibilities are. Also, if parents are involved in any way, their responsibilities should be included. You will probably find that students take the program more seriously if it is written in the form of a contract, especially if it involves their agreeing to the terms of the contract by signing it. Contracts can be made visually appealing, which helps make the program seem more fun. Here is an example of a contract used by a fifth-grade teacher.

BEN'S CONTRACT

I agree to work toward these goals:

Complete my math assignment during math period with no more than two reminders

Do the work neatly

Turn in the assignment at the end of the period

If I meet my goals, I will earn: **15 minutes on the computer**

If I do not meet my goals, I will not earn: **computer time**

_____

Student's signature   Date

I agree to monitor Ben's goals and give him the reward, if earned.

_____

Teacher's signature   Date

This part of the contract is included if parents are involved:

I agree to check Ben's report card daily and provide rewards at home when earned.

_____

Parent's signature   Date

SELF-MONITORING AND SELF-EVALUATION

Most of the programs discussed thus far have involved the teacher monitoring and evaluating students' behavior. However, the student can also be taught to monitor his or her own behavior. This skill is very important for students with ADHD since they are often impulsive and unaware of their own behavior and its impact on others. Researchers studying self-monitoring have found that having children earn rewards for accurate self-evaluations and positive behavior can be more effective than just having the teacher reward the positive behavior. In fact, research shows that the act of counting and recording one's own behavior tends to move the behavior in a positive direction. Increasing the students' awareness of their own behavior can be done informally (e.g., "How do you think you did today?") or as part of a formal program. One formal program used with students with ADHD is called "Match Game" (Hinshaw, Henker, & Whalen, 1984). This procedure involves having students rate their own behavior using descriptions, points, or colors over designated time periods. Younger children can rate more accurately when the rating categories are broad, so matching colors (not points) is recommended for them. Points should be reserved for older children (fourth grade and up). Extra points or a bonus are earned for ratings that match the teacher's ratings.

In the sample on the next page, only one target behavior is used (although you can have several target behaviors). The student first provides his or her rating in the upper left corner of the box. Afterward, the teacher gives his or her rating in the lower right corner of the box. If they match, bonus points are earned. If they do not match, the teacher rating is the one counted toward the reward.

Name: _____

Day: _____

I followed the class rules today.

8:30–10:00	10:00–11:30	11:30–1:00	1:00–2:30
S T	S T	S T	S T

0 = Not so good, didn't follow the rules
1 = OK, followed most of the rules
2 = Great, followed all of the rules

Matches:
Total points earned: _____

Teacher signature: _____

Other programs use a broader rating scale (e.g., 0–5 points) and the student keeps the points if their rating was within one point of the teacher rating, earns a bonus point for an exact match, or fails to earn points if their ratings deviate by more than one point.

Some teachers have students rate themselves more often as a prompt to stay on task and working. They might set a timer at random intervals and have the student check a box when the timer goes off if they have been working during that time or write down a 0 if they had not. Teachers can give their rating below the student's rating.

I WAS DOING MY WORK:							
Student							
Teacher							

Once children learn the system, they are awarded points only when their behavior is good and their rating matches the teacher's rating. With practice, students as young as 7 or 8 can learn to rate their own behavior accurately.

In one study, a group contingency was combined with self-management to decrease inappropriate talking in class. For this program, students worked together in small groups. To increase group cohesion, all students gave their group a name. Each group had a chart in the middle of its table to monitor the group's behavior. The chart was divided into green, blue, and red sections. Five black dots were adhered to the chart with Velcro tabs. One dot was to be moved by the student from the green to the blue section whenever "talking-out" occurred. If the child did not move the dot within 10 seconds, the teacher moved the dot to the red section. Students also monitored their behavior on individual sheets divided into two columns—one for the number of dots the student moved himself or herself and one for the times the teachers moved the dots. Rewards from a student-selected menu (most popular rewards: free time, sports and games) were earned for groups retaining at least one dot in the green section. Students were trained in all of the procedures, quizzed on the rules, and coached on how not to "gang up" on students having a bad day. Students discussed how they did during the first five minutes of each day by asking themselves: "What did we do well?" "What could we do better?" This system decreased the talking-out of students with ADHD during lessons to almost zero occurrences (Davies & Witte, 2000).

Students can also use checklists, such as the one shown at the right, to monitor their behavior. These kinds of self-monitoring checklists have been used successfully to improve organizational skills, as described in Chapter 2.

SELF RATINGS:

- Did I get started on time?
- Am I following directions?
- Am I working quietly?
- Did I turn in my completed work?

While older students can use checklists to monitor their behavior, younger children can learn to self-monitor using "countoons." These are cartoon versions of recording systems. They include a frame with a picture of the desired, and sometimes undesired, behaviors (e.g., a picture of themselves raising their hand or doing their work), a frame with a numerical count, and then a frame that depicts the reward they will earn if they meet their goal. Children give themselves a numerical rating of their own performance based on how many times they showed the target behavior (Daly & Ranalli, 2003).

When student ratings are consistently accurate, teacher ratings can be gradually faded and, for some students, rewards can be based on their self-ratings. However, teachers will still need to monitor the student ratings periodically (e.g., via random matching checks). Without monitoring, students can become overly lenient with their self-evaluations! You might also try having students predict how they think they will do before the activity and then see if their actual behavior matches their prediction (see sample on the next page). Having students make predictions can encourage positive behavior during the day (especially since most kids predict very successful days)!

FADING REWARD PROGRAMS

To maintain the gains of your reward program, you'll want to remove the program gradually and only after the behavior goals have been stable for at least several weeks or more. To fade a program, try the following:

- If you are using a token economy, reduce the frequency of token checks (e.g., from three times per day to once per day). This number can be further reduced (e.g., to once per week) as the student is successful.

- Modify the frequency and type of back-up rewards. For example, rewards can be given at the end of the week or every two weeks, instead of every day.

- Use fewer tangible rewards such as stickers or toys and use more activities and privileges instead.

- Have students earn their way off the reward program. Tell them that if they meet their goals for a certain period of time (at least several weeks), the program will be stopped. For older children, you may also require that the student continue to show accurate self-monitoring as the program is being faded.

CLASSROOM CHALLENGE
WITH STUDENT PREDICTIONS

Name: _____

Day: _____

Each category rated as follows: 2 = Great!!
                                     1 = Fair; needed 1 or 2 reminders
                                     0 = Unsatisfactory

Target Behavior: attends to class discussions

9:00–11:00	11:00–12:30	12:30–2:30
Student prediction	Student prediction	Student prediction
Teacher evaluation	Teacher evaluation	Teacher evaluation

Target Behavior: gets along with peers

9:00–11:00	11:00–12:30	12:30–2:30
Student prediction	Student prediction	Student prediction
Teacher evaluation	Teacher evaluation	Teacher evaluation

Target Behavior: completes assigned work

9:00–11:00	11:00–12:30	12:30–2:30
Student prediction	Student prediction	Student prediction
Teacher evaluation	Teacher evaluation	Teacher evaluation

Total points for a Great day: 15–18

Total points for a Fair day: 12–14

Total points for an Unsatisfactory day: 11 or less

Bonus for matching: 2

Total points earned: _____   _____
                                        Teacher's signature

THE PRUDENT USE OF NEGATIVE CONSEQUENCES

Positive consequences, no matter how extravagant, usually do not get rid of the need for negative consequences. This may be especially true for impulsive and aggressive behavior and for very persistent or serious problems. The use of verbal corrective feedback (reprimands) was discussed in an earlier section. However, students with ADHD often don't seem to be as responsive to such feedback as other students. They often need back-up negative consequences in addition to the reprimand. This section describes the prudent use of three negative consequences—response cost, work tasks, and time-out. Regardless of which particular strategies you use, punishment is most effective when it is brief, immediate, calm, and meaningful, and when lots of praise and rewards are given for positive behaviors.

USING RESPONSE COST

Response cost refers to the process of taking away privileges, tokens, or activities as a consequence for misbehavior. When certain guidelines are followed, this has proved to be one of the most effective negative consequences for children with ADHD.

There are many ways to set up response cost systems. For example, you might set up a system whereby students lose minutes from a scheduled 20-minute free activity period at the end of each day for each aggressive act. Students who have no aggressive behavior earn the entire 20 minutes. Each aggression may result in a loss of five minutes of free time, so a student who is aggressive twice loses ten minutes of free time. One teacher set up a response program using a music box to keep track of when students were following the rules. Whenever rules were not being followed, music was played. The number of minutes of music left at the end of the week corresponded to the number of minutes of free time earned by the whole class.

Another response cost approach involves giving students tokens at the beginning of the day. Tokens are then lost for certain misbehaviors. At the end of the day, children are "costed" based on the number of tokens they have lost. For example, a student might lose one minute of recess for every token lost. Another way to do this would be to have the student earn privileges based on the number of tokens kept. A teacher of a third-grade class gave one of her students five points to start the day (see report on page 111), and every time the child called out she lost a point. For each point the child still had at the end of the morning, she earned two minutes on the computer.

```
┌─────────────────────────────────────────────────────────┐
│                  BEHAVIOR REPORT                         │
│                                                          │
│  Name: _____ Day: _____      │
│                                                          │
│  Kept hands and feet to self:   1   2   3   4   5        │
│                                                          │
│  Total points kept: _____ X 2 = _____ minutes      │
│                                           computer time  │
│                                                          │
│  Teacher's signature: _____   │
│                                                          │
└─────────────────────────────────────────────────────────┘
```

Another system developed by Rapport, Murphy, & Bailey in 1980 involves using "flip cards." Flip cards are made from 20 hole-punched index cards that are attached by a ring. They are numbered from 1 to 20. One set is kept at the child's desk and another at the teacher's. At the beginning of the day, the child starts off with the 20 card on top. This represents 20 minutes of some privileged activity, such as recess. Each time the child breaks a rule, a card is flipped back so there is a visual reminder of how much time he or she has left for recess.

Some teachers use a color-card system whereby each student starts the day with a certain color card (often the color cards are kept in pockets or affixed with Velcro on a chart in class). When the student breaks a rule or gets a warning for behavior, the color card for that student is changed and a consequence may be given. With each successive infraction, the color card is changed (up to three or four colors are used) and another consequence may be given. To prevent bankruptcy early in the day in which all color cards are changed and the student has nothing left to work for, it is recommended that you have several opportunities for "fresh starts" during the day, especially for more problematic students. This is easily done by having colors start over each period (or several times a day). Students won't be able to change the color earned during preceding periods, but they can still work for a "better" color in later periods. Color earnings are totaled once per day and exchanged for a reward. In a study using response cost with kindergarten general-education students (Barkley et al., 2000), color earnings were totaled twice a day—once at the end of the morning and once at the end of the day—and exchanged for activity rewards. Those with mostly reds earned the most preferred activities, those with several yellows earned less preferred activities, and those with a blue earned the least preferred activities. The program was faded successfully over the course of the school year by gradually reducing feedback periods from twice per day to once a week, removing the chart from the class, and eliminating weekly rewards.

When using a cost system involving a loss of time to engage in a group activity, delaying access to the desired activity can be more effective than ending the student's participation early. In this approach, students wait a period of time before being allowed to start an activity, or more formally, students pay back time at the beginning of a desired activity (recess, after school). Note that even as little as one minute can be effective. However, be cautious when using loss of activity time as a consequence. Only a part of the activity (e.g., recess) should be lost and the effects of this consequence need to be closely monitored since it presents a risk if it is not used properly. If a student shows no or minimal improvement and ends up continually losing activities such as recess, the program should be adjusted since adverse effects from the removal of the activity could occur. Children may develop a reputation as the one who is always benched and also will lose out on opportunities for socialization with peers as well as physical exercise. If a student loses more than half the desired activity, it is probably not working and another approach should be tried.

Many teachers like to use response cost with a reward-based token economy. In this arrangement, a student can both earn tokens and lose tokens, as in the example below.

Using response cost to reduce misbehavior in the cafeteria:
In one large elementary school (700 students), a schoolwide program was implemented during lunchtime, a period rife with disciplinary referrals. Class lunchtimes were staggered so that up to 16 classes were in the cafeteria at one time. The school identified eight rules, including: treat people with kindness and respect, do all you can to make the school a safe place, treat property with care and respect, listen to all school staff, and use acceptable school language and voice. At the beginning of each lunch period, classes were given six lottery tickets. Throughout the lunch period, lottery tickets were lost for violations of school rules. Students could also earn additional bonus lottery tickets for following the rules during several random checks (bonus tickets could not be taken away). Class tickets were entered into a daily school lottery. Each morning, two class winners were drawn from the previous day's remaining tickets and those classes earned a privilege such as extra recess time or a walk outside. School staff also congratulated the students throughout the day. This program greatly reduced rule violations

during the lunch period, although generalization of gains to settings without the program did not occur (Fabiano et al., 2008).

Response cost versus reward: Many teachers wonder whether it is best to use response cost or a reward program. In other words, is it best to have students start with all their points (or reward) and then lose some of them when problems occur, or is it better to have students start with nothing and have them earn the reward? Research studies show that both procedures can be effective (Pfiffner et al., 2006). Response cost may be especially effective for aggressive and impulsive behavior since the student receives very immediate feedback directly related to the problem. For other behaviors, reward programs may be indicated. As an example, when trying to increase work productivity, it may be better to have students earn activities and privileges for completing their work, rather than losing privileges for not completing work. In this arrangement, a student who fails to complete work ends up not earning the privilege rather than losing the privilege. Framing programs in the positive way may decrease oppositional reactions. Consider the teacher's response in each of these approaches:

> "You didn't complete your work so you don't earn free time today"
>
> *vs.*
>
> "You didn't complete your work, so you lost your free time today."

The latter wording may be more likely to induce arguments in some children. The decision about whether to use response cost or rewards also depends on the student. Some students are easily demoralized by losing points; others like the idea of starting out with all their points at the beginning of the day,

RESPONSE COST MAY BE ESPECIALLY EFFECTIVE FOR AGGRESSIVE AND IMPULSIVE BEHAVIOR SINCE THE STUDENT RECEIVES VERY IMMEDIATE FEEDBACK DIRECTLY RELATED TO THE PROBLEM.

■ ■ ■

**TIPS**

USING RESPONSE COST

1. Don't use this procedure arbitrarily. Plan in advance what behaviors will result in a loss and apply the consequence consistently. Make sure the student understands what behaviors will result in a "cost."

2. Use one warning before taking away the privilege. This helps the student learn the system and is generally associated with less defiance or complaints of unfairness. An "if . . . then" statement works well, for example: "If you don't start your work, then you will lose some recess time."

3. When students are very angry, use an empathy statement to defuse the anger: "I know it is hard to stop in the middle of your game, but it is time to clean up."

4. Don't give more than one warning.

5. Incremental, rather than all-or-none, losses work well. For example, rather than losing all of recess, the student loses a certain number of minutes of recess based on the severity of the infraction.

6. Make sure the privileges or activities lost are meaningful to the student. For example, although most students would mind losing recess, some would prefer to stay inside. For those students, select another activity.

7. Stay calm. Don't use inflammatory language. Don't argue or lecture. Don't get too emotional or spend too much time trying to explain yourself.

8. When possible, try to ignore whining and oppositional verbal statements. Provide consequences only for actual noncompliance. Sometimes expecting a student to change both behaviors at once is too much.

9. Not giving enough tokens to start with is one of the most common mistakes that teachers make with response cost. Also, set fair, realistic goals. After the student has been successful, the goals can be increased. An occasional day of losing all tokens may be effective, but if it is a pattern, the goal is too high.

10. Be sure to notice and comment on positive behavior. Using response cost sometimes results in more attention to negative behavior. Don't let this happen.

rather than starting without any points. In many cases, the combination of rewards and response costs is the most powerful approach.

USING WORK TASKS

Another procedure for handling misbehavior such as defiance, aggression, or damaging property is assigning the student work tasks. This can prevent escalation of negative behavior and is a tool for helping the child regain self-control. One effective work task in use in the UCI-CDC school program

Name: _____

Day: _____

1. ☐ ☐ ☐ ☐ ☐ ☐ ☐ ☐ ☐ ☐

2. ☐ ☐ ☐ ☐ ☐ ☐ ☐ ☐ ☐ ☐

3. ☐ ☐ ☐ ☐ ☐ ☐ ☐ ☐ ☐ ☐

4. ☐ ☐ ☐ ☐ ☐ ☐ ☐ ☐ ☐ ☐

5. ☐ ☐ ☐ ☐ ☐ ☐ ☐ ☐ ☐ ☐

involves administering simple, boring, purposeless marking tasks upon the occurrence of problem behavior. This task involves the student drawing a diagonal line through a series of ten small boxes on a sheet of paper.

Another version of the task involves the student copying a series of numbers. Students can earn tasks for misbehavior, or they might earn tasks for not going to time-out promptly. Students may earn 5 tasks for certain infractions, 10 or even 20 tasks for more severe infractions. The teacher might say: "You're not following directions to go to time-out; that will be five tasks." If misbehavior continues, tasks are added by simply saying: "You are earning more tasks." When the child is sitting properly (at his or her seat or a special chair in the room used for doing tasks), he or she is given the task sheets to complete (they can be given one at a time). When the task sheets are complete, the teacher checks them for accuracy (lines must be diagonal) and then discards them. Although this is a writing task of sorts, it has not been found to negatively influence a child's interest in academic work.

USING TIME-OUT

Time-out means time away from positive reinforcement. Time-out involves removing the student from opportunities to earn positive reinforcement such as fun activities, peer attention, and teacher attention for a brief period of time. There are many ways to use time-out, such as removing work or materials from the student, or removing the student from preferred areas in the classroom to a time-out area. Another variation involves removing the opportunity to earn tokens for a period of time. One example of the latter is the Good Behavior Clock (Kubany, Weiss, & Sloggett, 1971). A clock runs whenever a student is on task, but is stopped for a short period of time when a student is off task or disruptive. While the clock is running, students can earn tokens or other rewards, but they are not eligible for earning rewards when the clock is stopped.

Class behavior management program combining time-out, response cost, and rewards: Valerie Bonacci, a teacher at Middlesex Elementary School, Carlisle, Pennsylvania, combines rewards and punishments in a behavior management program for her third-graders. This is how it works. The class has five rules: keep hands and feet to self, be respectful, ask teacher for permission to leave seat, raise hand to ask a question, and follow directions the first time. Student names are written on wooden craft sticks and placed in colored pockets (one for boys and one for girls) on a chart at the back of the class. The colored pockets are green, yellow, gray, and red. All students start the day with their name stick in the green pocket. If they stay in the green pocket all day, they get a "Bonacci buck," or B buck, at the end of the day. The first time a student breaks a rule during the day, he or she gets a warning, but the stick stays in the green pocket. A second rule infraction results in "take 5" which means the child moves to a designated desk at the back of the class, moves his or her stick to the yellow pocket, and turns a sand timer over for two to three minutes. When the time is up, the student returns to his or her seat. Following a third infraction, the student is instructed to "take 5 and fix it." This means the student needs to move the stick to the gray pocket, sit at the designated desk, and write down in a behavior book (located at the desk) what class rule was broken and how to fix it. Should a fourth infraction occur, the student has to "take 5 and fix it at recess." This means that the student must move the stick to the red pocket and lose recess, during which time he or she must write down the rule that was broken and how to will fix the problem. In addition, a note goes home to the parent about the problem.

USING TIME-OUT

TIPS

1. Select a time-out procedure. Common options include removing work materials, removing the opportunity to earn tokens or other rewards, or removing the student to an area in class that is free from reinforcing activities. A cubicle in the corner of the class works well.

2. Select a length of time. Usually two to three minutes is good to start. Extra time up to ten minutes may be added for students who refuse to go to time-out right away. An alternative is to start with five or ten minutes and then reduce the time (e.g., in half) if the student goes right away.

3. Select "back-up" consequences for failure to take a time-out or failure to follow time-out rules. Giving work tasks or taking away a privilege can be effective. For every minute a child refuses to go to time-out, he or she may have one minute after school or one minute off recess or one task. For rule violations during time-out (e.g., talking back, leaving the time-out area), points or privileges can be taken away.

4. Decide what behaviors will result in time-out. Common behaviors for time-out include aggression, repeated noncompliance, destruction of property, or general out-of-control behavior.

5. Describe the process to the student: "You have been doing a lot of hitting. We're going to start using time-out for hitting. That means whenever you hit or pretend to hit someone, you will have to go to the time-out chair at the back of the class."

6. Implement the procedure consistently, immediately, and calmly. Limit your talking to the student while he or she is in time-out. If the student is following time-out rules, don't say anything to the student. If the student is noncompliant and disruptive during time-out, calmly and briefly tell the student that he or she is earning work tasks or extra time, or losing privileges (e.g., for every minute of noncompliance during time-out, student loses one minute of recess or earns one minute of after-school detention). Do not argue with the student.

7. Classmates should be encouraged to ignore students in time-out. Interactions should get a negative consequence.

8. When time-out is over, don't discuss it with the student. Simply give the student a direction as to what to do and reinforce the next appropriate behavior. Too much talking after time-out could end up reinforcing the problem.

Bonacci also keeps a list of students in the yellow, gray, and red pockets at the front of the class. To keep kids motivated when their stick ends up in the yellow pocket, she allows them to earn partial bucks (e.g., Bonacci 50 cents) if they stay yellow. She has a list of rewards posted with the purchase price (in B bucks) listed for each. Popular rewards include sitting in the teacher's chair, taking shoes off, sitting at the teacher's desk, eating in the classroom with a friend, and choosing a small toy from a treasure chest. She finds that most days only one or two children end up on yellow; all the rest stay green. She attributes part of the success of this program to the fact that she spends the first few weeks of the school year going over the rules of the program very carefully—modeling exactly how it looks to be following the rules and then having students role-play the examples. In addition to these individual rewards, she also utilizes group rewards. She has a huge piggy bank in her class. Students earn plastic quarters for a variety of behaviors (walking quietly to special activities, following direction and rules). The quarters exchange for B bucks, which can be exchanged for class rewards such as eating in class and watching a movie.

Schoolwide programs: Several schoolwide programs have been developed that combine many of the ideas (e.g., praise, daily report cards, homework organizational tools) presented in earlier sections of this book. For example, the Academic and Behavioral Competencies (ABC) Program was developed and implemented at North Lincoln Elementary School in Alliance, Ohio, and at urban Early Childhood Centers in Buffalo, New York, public schools to improve disruptive behavior and academic performance. The program included increasing praise to students, use of consistent schoolwide rules monitored daily using class rosters, homework assignment sheets (signed by parents), daily positive notes home for students who followed rules, weekly fun enrichment activities and special privileges (e.g., "Behavior Honor Roll") for students who earned positive notes home, time-out for serious misbehavior, response cost ticket system during lunch, social skill review in class and at lunch, and individualized programs for students if needed (Pelham et al., 2005). Teachers, parents, and students were all very favorable about the program and reported improvements in student behavior.

CHAPTER 5

THE SCHOOL-HOME CONNECTION: PARENT AND TEACHER PARTNERSHIPS

WORKING TOGETHER

Promoting a teacher-parent team spirit of cooperation is one of the best things you can do for an ADHD student. You will find that you will need to be more involved with parents of students with ADHD, at least at the beginning of the year. Let parents know when problems first arise.

Parents can be a wonderful resource. Many are eager to become involved and support your efforts at school. Unfortunately not all parents provide the time and effort needed to effectively work with students with ADHD. Some are ill-equipped to handle their child's behavior and are overly punitive. Others are multiply stressed by life situations such as divorce, financial difficulties, unemployment, lengthy work hours, and family conflict. It is important to recognize that most parents of ADHD children have experienced the same kinds of difficulties with their child as you have. They are often equally frustrated and overwhelmed. In all likelihood, they have been made aware of their child's misbehavior and failure on many occasions over the years. Previous teachers have probably complained about the student, as have relatives, friends, and even strangers in supermarkets and at parks. They may feel blamed for their child's problems and they may react defensively.

COMMUNICATE HOPE.

■ ■ ■

They may seem to blame you for their child's problems. You may find yourself wondering if poor parenting is the root of the problem. *Remember: ADHD is not caused by poor parenting*—in fact, many parents with ADHD youngsters may have ADHD themselves. Nor is it caused by particular teaching techniques. Don't give up too early with an uncooperative parent. Try to be patient, non-defensive, and encouraging when meeting with parents. Many will "come around" when other crises in their lives resolve or when they see your consistent efforts with their child.

What's the best way to communicate with parents and enlist their support in the educational process? Foster a team spirit. Show your commitment to working with the student. Stay problem focused. Don't blame. Point out students' strengths. Communicate hope.

Keep parents informed about your class procedures. Give parents a list of classroom rules and procedures at the beginning of the year. Have them sign and return the list to you. Throughout the school year, keep parents abreast of any changes. You can also let them know how they can be helpful at home with their child's education. Tips about good books to read, educational programs to watch, places to go, and how they can best be involved with homework are all helpful.

HOMEWORK

Homework is usually a struggle for families of children with ADHD. Work that takes some students 30 minutes to do may take over an hour for a student with ADHD. Lengthy homework often leads to heated family arguments and becomes demoralizing for students with ADHD. Don't set families up; be realistic in the amount of work assigned for homework. Don't send incomplete classwork home as homework. If a student doesn't complete work in class, it's unlikely that it will be done with much success at home (unless the parent does it). For kindergartners and first graders, 10 minutes of homework per night is plenty (if any is assigned at all). For second and third graders, 30 minutes should be the limit. For fourth through sixth graders, one or two 30-minute blocks of homework per night is probably sufficient.

At the beginning of the year, be clear with parents and students about what your expectations are for homework. What are your goals for homework? Should parents help the student? How much? What kind of homework will be assigned each night? How long should it take?

HOMEWORK EXPECTATIONS FORM

Teacher Name: _____

Student Name: _____

How do students find out what the homework assignment is for daily, weekly, and long-term projects (if assigned)?
How should students keep track of the homework assignment? Do they write it down*, or do you? If a planner is used, what are the components that students should use each day? * If students write down the homework themselves, remember that it may be necessary for you to verify its accuracy each day.
Should parents help child with homework? If so, how should they help?
Should parents correct homework? (Give answers if they correct homework.)
How important is neatness?
How long should homework take?
What changes, if any, do you want for this student's homework performance?

It is also important for parents to know whether homework is checked for the amount done or for accuracy as well. Knowing this will provide them with information about how important it is for them to correct their child's homework. The form on page 121 is meant to serve as a tool to convey your homework expectations to parents.

To help make homework expectations explicit, Donna Hall, a third-grade teacher at Culverdale Elementary School in Irvine, California, distributes the homework contract shown on the next page to all families at the beginning of each school year.

Hall adds a bonus for students who complete homework assignments. At the bottom of this contract she states: "Completed work will be rewarded on the last Friday of the month. Students who have missed no more than four assignments will qualify for the special movie. Those who do not qualify will work on independent work."

Be creative when assigning homework.

➲ Use Internet postings of complete homework assignments if you can. The posting should include the complete assignment (daily assignments and longer-term projects), the materials needed, and the due dates. It is still crucial that you review the homework assignment with students each day in order to clearly present what they need to do and to answer questions. Some teachers also allow students to e-mail them if they have questions.

➲ Use homework assignment sheets if Internet postings are not available or incomplete. A daily or weekly assignment sheet listing assignments for each day of the week can be used. Alternatively, but with greater chance of error, students can write down assignments (see page 124). The student writes down the assignment as well as the materials needed and due date. The teacher checks to make sure the assignment is written correctly and signs the form. The parent can also sign the form after the assigned homework is completed. Be sure to give students time to write down the assignment at the beginning or end of the day (or period). When you give assignments, be as clear as you possibly can. Make a point to go over the assignment thoroughly. Have students repeat the assignment to make sure they understand.

HOMEWORK CONTRACT

Dear Parents:

To insure that all persons concerned will understand my policy for homework, I would like you to discuss the following contract with your child and then have both of you sign it. I have previously reviewed this with your child in class. If you have any questions, please contact me or have your child see me at school.

As the teacher, I will provide:

- Instructional background for the work
- Materials needed in student mailboxes
- Reminder of the work on the homework chart

Teacher's signature: _____

As the parent, I will:

- Provide a quiet work area
- Provide a designated time for homework
- Monitor work as needed (watch neatness)
- Show pleasure over completed work and initial the work
- Write a note to my teacher if the child was confused about the assignment

Parent's signature: _____

As the student, I will:

- Try my very best on my own
- Use my neatest handwriting
- Turn my work in on time
- Have my parent initial my finished work
- Let my teacher know if I had any problems
- Show all my school work to my parents each night
- Have my parents sign any important papers and return them to school

Student's signature: _____

⮩ Consider using a homework buddy system. Pair the student with ADHD with a conscientious student who consistently completes homework. Have that student check in with the buddy at the end of the day to be sure the ADHD student has the accurate assignment and all materials needed.

Use self-monitoring checklists to help students remember what to take home. Here's a basic reminder checklist for homework or "Things I need to take home":

⮩ Is the homework folder in front of a binder, with homework to be completed on the left side and homework to be turned in on right side?

⮩ Are assignments and tests recorded accurately in the planner?

⮩ Are there any papers to take home?

⮩ Are there any papers to return to school?

To remind students to check their homework list, use a reminder card. One student found that attaching a jiggly key chain to his backpack zipper worked as a good reminder—when he picked up his backpack to go home, the chain jiggled, reminding him to check his homework list. For tips on backpack organization see Chapter 2.

HOMEWORK ASSIGNMENT PLANNER					
Week of: _____	Assignment	Books and materials needed	Due date	Teacher's signature	Parent's signature
Monday					
Tuesday					
Wednesday					
Thursday					
Friday					

Be sure not to neglect the importance of checking students' completed homework and providing feedback as soon as possible! If feedback is very delayed (or does not occur at all), students may end up not taking homework very seriously.

Help parents encourage homework completion. Many parents have difficulty getting their children to do homework and would benefit from your suggestions. First of all, emphasize the importance of their staying informed about the homework assignments. They should be encouraged to check to make sure the assignment planner is complete and signed by the teacher each day (or check the homework Web site) and that the proper materials have been brought home. Let parents know that having a set time and place to do the work is usually a good idea. The time should be selected to fit into the family schedule. You might want to give students the homework well in advance of the due date (give homework due on Friday at the beginning of the week). Parents and students can then choose which nights the student is to complete the homework so that planned family activities and sports don't have to be sacrificed. Give parents and students an idea of how long homework should take. If it is taking much longer than that, set a time limit. Consider reducing the workload. The place to do homework should be one in which the child feels comfortable and not overly distracted. Tell parents to allow their children to have short work breaks (often a necessity for children with ADHD since they have trouble focusing their attention for long). Encourage parents to monitor and check their child's work (but not do the work for him or her). Advise parents how you would like corrections to be handled.

Parents should also make a point to reward their children for getting the work done. You might want to give parents suggestions about rewards to use based on what you see that works in class (e.g., praise, privileges, activities, stickers, chore passes). Since productivity is usually the problem, tell parents to set up rewards for the amount and accuracy of work completed, not just simply for the student looking like they are doing the work. Sometimes it's also helpful for the parent to serve as a good role model and schedule to work on some "homework-like" tasks during the time the child is working on homework. *Most important:* Advise parents that homework can easily fall through the cracks if they aren't involved.

Some parents also may be encouraged to serve in a tutoring role with their child. Parents can be provided with specific skills for working with their child and the curriculum in the context of homework time. Such an approach has been shown to improve reading performance, although it is probably most effective with children who are generally compliant with their parents. In many cases, children work better with non-parents!

PARENTS SHOULD ALSO MAKE A POINT TO REWARD THEIR CHILDREN FOR GETTING THE WORK DONE.

■ ■ ■

Other tips include the following:

- ➲ Have a second set of books/workbooks for home use.

- ➲ If the child is not doing homework at home, allow time for it to be completed at school (e.g., end of school day).

- ➲ If a child is doing well in a particular subject, consider reducing or omitting homework in that area (e.g., spelling tests for words spelled correctly in practice test).

- ➲ Give homework passes for completing all homework for a specified number of days. Give students a night off homework as a reward for doing the work and getting the parent signature.

- ➲ Have a homework partner to help record and check accuracy of the assignment and put proper materials in the folder. Homework partners should be very organized and dependable.

- ➲ Have students clean out their backpacks on a weekly basis.

Sample homework procedure with school reward: David Agler assigns homework on Wednesdays that is due the following Tuesday (giving students the option of completing homework over the weekend). He includes a recommended schedule outlining when to do what, but this can be flexible depending on the child's schedule. The parent provides a global rating indicating how well their child (1–5 in a box) used time effectively, completed the assignment, tried to complete the work by himself or herself, was neat, and asked questions when he or she needed help. Students earn homework tickets based on the parent rating; these are entered into a daily drawing during morning meetings each day. Parents are also told that children will do the homework at school the next day if it is not done at home. However, the teacher advises parents that children will do almost anything in the heat of the moment to escape homework, so that warning them that they will have to complete it at school the next day may not work to improve their homework skills.

LONG-TERM PROJECTS

Some students can be successful with daily routine assignments but end up not keeping track of long-term projects, and parents may never find out about them. Take special care that students write down their long-term projects and due dates. Give parents the tip sheet on the next page so they can assist their child.

THE DAILY SCHOOL-HOME REPORT CARD

The daily school-home report card is an excellent intervention for many students with ADHD. It involves parents giving consequences at home based on the teacher's report of the child's performance at school. Teacher reports can be notes or more formal report cards with a list of the target behaviors and a rating for each behavior. The report card is usually sent home on a daily basis at first. Sometimes report cards are sent only on "good" days (i.e., when behavior or academic goals are met); in other cases report cards are sent on both "good" and "bad" days. After a period of success, the report cards can sometimes be faded to weekly, biweekly, and monthly, and, finally, to the reporting intervals typically used in school. However, in many cases, students with ADHD benefit from having a daily or weekly report card in place for the entire school year. The daily report card, or DRC, is considered an evidence-based intervention for ADHD and is recommended by the United States Department of Education as an effective educational practice for students with ADHD (DOE, 2004). For more details regarding teacher-parent communication and daily report cards see Mary Lou Kelley's book *School-Home Notes*, or go to the Web site Center for Children and Families (ccf.buffalo.edu/resources_downloads.php).

Advantages of using a school-home report card:

- ➲ Facilitates home-school communication
- ➲ Gives students more frequent feedback than usually occurs in class
- ➲ Prompts parents to reinforce good behavior
- ➲ Provides the type and quality of reinforcers that are greater at home than at school
- ➲ Requires less time for teacher than many in-class interventions
- ➲ Can be used as a record of student's progress
- ➲ Facilitates early detection of the need for problem solving

Cautions in using a school-home report card. Do not use a school-home report card if you are concerned about follow-through at home. Some parents do not have the skills necessary to reinforce consistently at home. In some cases, you may be concerned about overly punitive consequences. In these instances, consult with your school psychologist to try and locate a therapist who can provide assistance in child management skills for the family.

Also, don't use a school-home report card if the major problem is a learning disability or an academic deficit. Sometimes adding incentives can increase frustration in a child who simply does not understand the academic material. School-home report cards are most effective when problems are due to motivational or attention deficits.

Note that these programs require that students be able to delay gratification until they get home that day. For some students, this is not realistic. If behavior problems are severe, or if a student needs more immediate rewards, you will need to supplement the school-home report card with rewards in class.

Steps for designing a reporting system. The initial steps for setting up a school-home report card are much like those for setting up a token economy (since a school-home report card is essentially a token economy). Before meeting with the student and parents, identify a few target behavior goals you would like the child to achieve, collect a baseline rate of the behaviors, and set reasonable goals for the student. Then design a "rough draft" of a reporting system to use. Several variations of school-home report cards are given on pages 129–131.

Sample 1: Includes two target behaviors rated three times a day and a rating of work completion. Space is provided for writing down the homework assignment and home rewards, and for the parent's signature.

_____'s Day   Date _____

Stayed seated with no more than 3 reminders	8:30–10:00	10:00–11:30	11:30–1:00
Interrupted no more than 3 times			

Legend: 1 = yes   0 = no

% of work completed correctly

(90–100% = 4 points, 80–89% = 3 points, 70–79% = 2 points, less than 70% = 0 points)

Homework for tonight:

Teacher's signature:_____

Home Rewards:

9–10 points = basic and bonus privileges at home

7–8 points = basic privileges at home

less than 7 points = only inside activities at home
(no basic or bonus privileges)

Parent's signature: _____

Sample 2: Includes three target behaviors rated each period and two bonus target behaviors: one for remembering to ask the teacher for the rating at each time period (C. C. Notebook Bonus) and one for following the rules at recess (Recess Bonus).

Name: _____ Date: _____

CLASSROOM CHALLENGE

TARGET BEHAVIORS	TIME		
	Before Recess	Before Lunch	End of School
Asks for help when needed	0 1 2	0 1 2	0 1 2
Keeps hands and feet to self	0 1 2	0 1 2	0 1 2
Keeps materials organized	0 1 2	0 1 2	0 1 2
C. C. Notebook Bonus	0 1 2	0 1 2	0 1 2
Recess Bonus	Recess 1: 0 1 2	Recess 2: 0 1 2	Recess 3: 0 1 2
DAILY TOTAL	= _____ "STARS"		

POINT SCALE: 0 = Needs Improvement   1 = Okay   2 = Super Job

_____   _____
Teacher's signature   Parent's signature

Sample 3: Includes two target behaviors rated three times per day.

Name: _____ Date: _____

	Language arts	Math	Science
Follows directions with no more than 2 reminders	yes/no	yes/no	yes/no
Gets along with classmates	yes/no	yes/no	yes/no

Total yes's = _____

Teacher's signature: _____

Parent's signature: _____

Sample 4: Includes two target behaviors for earning points, and one target behavior that results in a loss of points—happy faces are crossed out for each instance of being out of seat without permission (token economy with response cost).

Name: _____ Date: _____		
Period/Time/Class	**Math**	**Language Arts**
Best effort during classwork (no reminders, nice handwriting, accurate work)	☹ ☺	☹ ☺
Asks for help when needed	☹ ☺	☹ ☺
Out of seat without permission	☺ ☺ ☺	☺ ☺ ☺
Total # of ☺		
Teacher's signature: _____ Parent's signature: _____		

Meeting with the parent and the student:

1. Bring your list of target behaviors, your baseline records and sample report card to the meeting. Meet alone with the parent first.

2. Open the meeting by setting the stage for cooperation. Point out the student's strengths and positive attributes.

3. Pinpoint specific problems in a non-blaming, non-ridiculing fashion.

4. Provide a rationale and describe the daily report card. Show samples of how one might look. The following is a script of how a teacher might present the report card system to a parent.

Teacher: Thank you for meeting with me today. I think it's best to meet early in the year so that we can make the year for Raul be the most successful it can be. First of all, I want to say that I have really enjoyed Raul's enthusiasm and participation in class discussions. He seems to be very bright and very energetic. But I am concerned about some problem behaviors. Raul seems to be having trouble completing his work, and also spends too much time socializing with other students in the class. I have tried moving his seat so he's away from his friends, but it doesn't seem to have solved the problem. I've also tried to make sure he understands the assignments. That doesn't seem to be a problem. At this point, it seems that he just is not motivated to complete the work. One thing that I have found works well in these cases is a daily school-home report card or school-home note. In this system, we set up a few goals for Raul each day, like completing his assignments and following the no-talking class rule. I keep track of his behavior in these two areas and send a note home to let you know how he did. If Raul did well, you would provide some reward for him at home. The reward might be something like special time with you, extra playtime with friends, extra TV time. If he didn't do well, he wouldn't get the reward. Here is an example of how the report card might look (*show copy*) and here is a list of some rewards you might consider using. I have found this procedure to be very effective for many kids. What do you think about it? Does it seem like something you might be able to do?

5. Advise the parent to use basic privileges, not expensive, elaborate rewards. Emphasize the advantages of using privileges and activities as rewards instead of always relying on tangible rewards (low cost, always on hand, renewable). Also, tell parents to avoid using rewards they cannot withhold if not earned. For example, if the whole family is going to the ball game over the weekend regardless of the child's behavior, they should not use the ball game as a reward. The negative consequence for poor ratings is usually not earning the reward. However, additional negative consequences (e.g., early bedtime, loss of playtime) can be applied for very poor ratings, assuming the parent has the skill to implement these kinds of consequences in a calm and not overly punitive fashion.

6. After the parent has agreed to the procedure, have the child join you and the parent. Mention some of the child's positive behaviors. Then describe your concerns to the child and the idea of using a daily report card. Involve the student in generating a menu of potential home rewards. You can give the child a copy of the list of rewards in this book. Set realistic criteria for earning a daily reward at home. As with other reward programs, the goals should be well within the reach of the child. If possible, you may also wish to include rewards at school.

7. Establish procedures for getting the card rated during the day. The DRC is most effective when teachers make the ratings right after the time period they are earned (not just the end of the day). When the program first starts, teachers should prompt the student and not wait until the student brings them the card to sign (most students cannot remember to get it signed at the beginning). Over time, older students can be given the responsibility for handing the card to the teacher for signing at the appropriate time (e.g., end of class period). You can consider rewarding the student for bringing the card to you without prompting by including this as a target behavior (and worth a token). Note, however, that some students may continue to need prompting to get the ratings.

8. Establish procedures for taking the card home and showing it to parents. Students are responsible for taking the card home and showing it to parents. A time for this should be established. Parents are responsible for delivering rewards if earned or withholding rewards if not earned. A visual reminder on the student's desk can be a useful prompt.

9. Have the student go through a "practice day" to make sure he or she understands the program. The student should be able to describe the specific target behaviors, the criteria, and the way the ratings on the card translate into rewards at home. Also make sure that the student has a place to carry the report

card between school and home. Make up a contract with the responsibilities of all parties and signatures.

10. Troubleshoot the following potential problems with parent and student:

⮑ What happens when the student forgets to bring the card to the teacher for a rating? The teacher should prompt the student. If this continues to happen, add bringing the card up to the teacher without a reminder as a target behavior.

⮑ What happens when the student forgets to bring the card home? The day is treated as if the goal was not achieved. This means the parent withholds the reward.

⮑ What happens when the student claims the teacher did not have time or refused to sign the card? The day is treated as if the goal was not achieved. Assure the parent that you will be available to sign the card. But be sure the student knows when to ask you.

⮑ What happens in the case of forgery or tampering? At a minimum, the day is treated as if the goal was not achieved. The parent may also wish to withhold an additional privilege or have the student write an apology note to the teacher for forging.

⮑ What happens when the schedule is changed or there is a substitute? Usually the program is not in effect when a substitute teacher is present. However, the student is still responsible for his or her behavior, and if any negative reports come home, rewards would be withheld, or consequences levied.

11. Start the program and follow through:

⮑ Make copies of the daily report card. It is useful to have the parent and child create the report cards at home. However, the program is often expedited if you make the copies.

⮑ Initially, provide the student with prompts for success. Remind the student to give you the card, and throughout the day, notice progress and comment on how well he or she is doing toward meeting the daily goal.

↪ Be positive. Encourage parents to focus on what their child did well each day. If problems occur, have parents ask their child what he or she might do to improve the next day.

↪ Be consistent.

12. Schedule a follow-up contact for one to two weeks after the initial meeting to check on the progress of the program. If all is well, this contact may be via a note, e-mail, or telephone call to the parent. If problems are continuing or if the card doesn't seem to be implemented as planned, try to schedule another meeting or telephone contact. These programs often need some modification.

On page 137 is a list of activities, privileges, and tangible rewards that parents may wish to use at home to reward the child for meeting daily, weekly, or longer-term goals. Remember that the most effective report cards are those where target goals are very specific (e.g., no more than three interruptions, at least four assignments completed) so that it is very clear what you want the child to do. Report cards that use very general, evaluative goals (e.g., be a good student) with feedback given only at the end of the day (or week) often don't work. The child should get feedback at least several times a day.

For one particularly difficult student, Mary Olvak, a second-grade teacher at PS 182, Bronx, New York, set up a report card with the initial goal being no more than six interruptions per half hour. As the student was able to do this, the goal was increased, so that over several months, the student was able to be successful with a goal set at no more than one interruption per half-hour period. At first, Olvak found monitoring the student's behavior every 15–30 minutes to be somewhat overwhelming. But she says that it didn't take long for her to find this procedure to be "absolutely easier" than constantly dealing with negative behavior. She also says that using this approach helped reduce her anger, since the focus is on giving the student factual feedback about his or her behavior (e.g., "That's more than three interruptions; no points for this period."), and not on winning a battle with the student.

Handling parent questions and concerns. Parents often have questions about the daily report card. Here are suggestions on how to respond to a few common questions or concerns.

Parent: I'm sure Kevin would like to earn some of these things. But don't you think he should be able to do his work without them? I'm worried that he'll only do the work for the reward.

Teacher: I understand your concern. But all kids need rewards. Right now, Kevin does not seem to be responding to the rewards in class that some of the other kids respond to, like getting good grades. This program would simply involve adding an extra incentive to make it very clear that doing well in school pays off. At the beginning, he may work primarily for the rewards, but over time, he should begin enjoying the satisfaction of doing a good job and getting good grades.

Parent: I don't get home until 7:00 every night, and I don't have much time to reward my child.

Teacher: Effective rewards often don't have to take much time. Consider a bedtime story or a 10-minute game with you. I have a feeling your child would really value this time with you even if it's only 10 minutes. It could make a big difference in his work at school.

Parent: I'm worried that my son will feel embarrassed or singled out with this report card.

Teacher: It may be hard for your son not to feel somewhat singled out. But this approach is meant to help him be more successful in school, which should help improve how he feels about himself. Also, we can make the report card as private as possible. He can come up at the end of class to get my signature or leave it for me at the beginning of the class and pick it up at the end. As he shows improvement, he can work his way off the contract.

Parent: What should I do if my son brings home a report card showing he had a bad day and didn't earn very many points?

Teacher: When your son brings home such a report, you might try asking him in a calm way about what did not go so well. But don't get into a long discussion about the problem. If your son refuses to take responsibility for the problem, don't keep pressing him to get a "confession." Just let it go. It's usually better not to dwell on the problem but to focus more on how he can improve—ask what he could work on to do better the next day. Also, don't overlook those things that did go well.

Whatever you do, be sure that your son does not get the reward he would have gotten if the report was a good one. Don't argue with your son over this or let him talk you out of it! The next morning, give him encouragement to have a good day. If you have any questions about what happened, feel free to contact me.

SUGGESTED HOME REWARDS

Daily	Weekly
Bedtime story	Arts/crafts
Bubble bath	Buy new DVD or CD or download
Chore pass	music for iPod
Computer time	Cooking
Food or drink treat after school	Eat out at restaurant
Game with parent	Get a new book
Help with cooking	Go bowling
Later bedtime	Go to beach or lake
Money	Go to video arcade
More playtime with friends	Grab bag (pick a toy from a bag)
Outside play	New hair clips
Practice sport with parent	Outing to spend money earned
Ride bike	Overnight with friend
Rollerblading	Pizza or other take-out food
Snack of choice	Rental movie
Special dessert	Trip to mall
Swimming	
Telephone privileges	**Monthly or longer**
Trip to park	Amusement park
TV time	New clothes
	Sporting goods

Research supports use of the DRC. Fabiano and colleagues (2009) evaluated the effectiveness of a daily report card compared to "business as usual" among a group of children with ADHD in special education placements. In the DRC condition, behavioral consultants met with the teacher to identify target behaviors for the DRC. A standard list of common target goals was provided. The teacher implemented the program for one week, then met again with the consultant to refine the target behaviors and modify the criteria for success based on the students' performance. At a third meeting, the DRC was fine-tuned, and the teacher was told of the home rewards provided by parents. IEP goals were figured into the DRC system. Ratings of behavior were made throughout the school day and the DRC was sent home with the children each day. (For examples of the DRCs used in this study see ccf.buffalo.edu. This Web site contains downloadable handouts on how to design and troubleshoot a DRC.) After the three initial meetings, the teachers met with the consultant monthly to provide feedback on the children's behavior—graphs of the DRC ratings were reviewed. Goals and target behaviors were modified as needed throughout the school year. Students in the business-as-usual group received an IEP and goals were set, but a DRC was not implemented. Results showed that by the end of the school year, children who received a DRC showed improved classroom behavior and completed more assigned work compared to children who did not receive a DRC but had an IEP and the usual accompanying interventions. They also were more successful in achieving their IEP goals. Academic achievement was not influenced by having a DRC, suggesting that academic remediation should also be included for students with academic skills deficits.

REVERSE DAILY REPORT CARD

Some teachers use a reverse system whereby they reward students at school for good behavior at home. The procedure for rewarding good homework behavior at school as described above is an example of this. Other behaviors targeted by parents can also be included, such as getting ready in the morning. In one program, when the child was successful, the parent sent in a note with the number of points earned and what they were earned for. The student was given a sticker on successful days so that other adults could ask about their success and provide even more positive attention. In another program, the teacher gave the student a slip of paper with the reward written in invisible ink—they used a special scratch-able pen to reveal what reward was earned (like a lotto scratcher).

INTEGRATED SCHOOL-HOME PROGRAMS

The Child Life and Attention Skills Program The Child Life and Attention Skills (CLAS) program was developed as a collaborative school-home program for children in the second through fifth grades with attention problems. The program has been adapted for children with hyperactivity, impulsivity, and behavioral concerns as well. It involves teachers and parents partnering to provide necessary environmental supports at school and at home. The program lasts for about 12 weeks and includes school (consultation with teachers), family (parenting skills groups), and child (skills groups) components which are integrated via joint teacher, parent, and child meetings and use of integrated behavioral programs in the classroom and playground and at home. As part of the program, teachers are provided with information about ADHD, as well as many of the behavioral interventions and classroom accommodations discussed in previous sections of this book. They meet with parents, students, and a mental health professional over the 12-week program to develop and implement a daily report card (called "Classroom Challenge"), like those discussed previously. Parents support the Classroom Challenge by providing daily and weekly rewards at home when students reach their goals. Parents attend 10 weekly group sessions with a mental health professional and learn techniques to promote social, behavioral, and academic development in their child. These include positive forms of communication, positive reinforcement, homework management skills, discipline, use of routines, and time management/organizational skills. Parents develop a home token economy ("Home Challenge") which is integrated with the Classroom Challenge for daily and weekly rewards at home. Students attend weekly skills groups where they are taught a series of skills focused on independence (homework/study skills, self-care skills, getting chores done, routines), and social skills (friendship making, handling teasing, good manners, accepting things they may not like, being a good sport, and problem solving). Groups can be held at the child's school or at a clinic. Celebratory parties are held for students and parents to sustain motivation and celebrate accomplishments made by the children at school and home.

The program has resulted in significant improvement in ADHD symptoms (attention, hyperactivity, impulsivity), problem behavior, and social and organizational skills. The program provides a model for how teachers, parents, and students can successfully work together for substantial gains at school and at home (Pfiffner et al., 2007).

PARENTS SUPPORT THE CLASSROOM CHALLENGE BY PROVIDING DAILY AND WEEKLY REWARDS AT HOME WHEN STUDENTS REACH THEIR GOALS.

■ ■ ■

CHAPTER 6

DECIDING WHICH PROCEDURES TO USE

You've identified the problems, and you're aware of the many options you have for dealing with them. How do you know what to do and when to do it? Here are some guidelines.

1. Start first with good teaching strategies (see Chapters 2 and 3). These strategies might include making sure that you have clear and consistently enforced rules, a predictable routine for the day, and prominently posted homework assignments, and that you are giving good directions, using your attention strategically, and involving students in the lessons.

2. Select a solution relevant to the problem at hand based on your assessment of what's setting it off and what's maintaining the problem. For example, if being around certain peers sets off the problem, consider moving the student's seat. If the student is bored and easily distracted during lessons, involve the student more often in the lesson. If the student misbehaves to get your attention, give attention to the student, but only when he or she is behaving well!

3. Don't just try to reduce problem behaviors. Always replace negative behaviors with positive ones.

4. Set up reward programs before using punishment.

5. Use developmentally appropriate strategies. Younger children usually need more frequent feedback, concrete rewards given right away, more prompting, and very simple, brief directions.

Older children can manage with a somewhat greater delay in receiving rewards and less frequent feedback (but not a lot less). They should be more actively involved in designing the program and take more responsibility for it, including monitoring their own behavior. They often respond well to contracts.

6. Decide what to do based on what's practical for you. Complicated programs are prone to inconsistency. If something is too hard or complicated, think about how you can simplify it to meet your needs as well as the needs of the student. Strategies need to be individualized for teachers just as they are for students! Try picking one strategy to work on or one setting (e.g., transition time) at a time before moving on to the next.

7. Think of interventions as "mini-experiments." Sometimes it is hard to know if something will work without trying it. Decide on an intervention, and then see what effect it has. Stick with an intervention for about one month or so (shorter if problems get consistently worse!). If improvement does not occur, begin another experiment with another intervention.

The checklist that follows summarizes many of the strategies presented in this book and can be used as a guide to select solutions. The strategies are divided into ten general areas related to specific strategies with sample problems relevant to each. However, keep in mind that most of the strategies are useful for many different problems. Likewise, many problems benefit from strategies in a combination of different areas. Refer to related book sections for more specific information about particular strategies.

TEACHER SELF-ASSESSMENT CHECKLIST

Area 1: Classroom Environment
Do I arrange the classroom environment to promote learning readiness?

⮌ Have student sit near the front of the class, away from distractions and near positive peer role models.

⮌ Keep classroom uncluttered and well organized.

⮌ Utilize visual aides to emphasize limits and rules.

Area 2: Teaching Styles

Do I use interactive teaching styles and techniques?

⮑ Actively involve students in lessons. If the class is not engaged, or answering questions appropriately, simplify your discussion and give more examples.

⮑ Use high-interest, multisensory, and hands-on approaches.

⮑ Have well-organized lesson plans.

⮑ Pace lectures for ability and attention span (shorten, limit downtime). Avoid spending a lot of class time writing on the board with your back to the class.

⮑ Frequently move around class when lecturing or monitoring independent seatwork to allow for scanning and feedback.

⮑ Provide immediate feedback regarding quality of work produced.

Area 3: Organizational Skills

Do I give tools to improve organizational skills?

⮑ Use daily assignment books.

⮑ Use written descriptions of daily and long-term assignments.

⮑ Use color-coded activities and assignment folders.

⮑ Use folder taped to the side of desk for completed papers.

⮑ Organize student desk/work space, have desk checks.

⮑ Assign study or homework buddy.

Area 4: Accommodations to Assignments

Do I make accommodations to assignments when the student is overwhelmed by lengthy or very effortful assignments and can't complete it in a reasonable amount of time?

⮑ Shorten assignments.

⮑ Allow use of word processors, spelling checks, and so on.

⮑ Allot extra time to complete tests, assignments.

⮑ Provide brief work breaks.

⮑ Break tasks into manageable, small parts.

⮑ Use student-selected projects in areas of interest.

Area 5: Class Rules

Do I use these guidelines for class rules?

➲ Keep rules simple; add new rules if needed.

➲ Generate rules with student input.

➲ Post rules in the front of the class.

➲ Use hand signs or other nonverbal prompts to remind kids of rules.

➲ State consequences for following and not following rules.

Area 6: Giving Directions

Do I use these guidelines for giving directions?

➲ Use statements (e.g., "You have a direction to . . ."), not questions.

➲ Give only one direction at a time.

➲ Be specific and brief.

➲ Give directions or admonitions in a neutral or positive tone of voice.

➲ Have student repeat direction to ensure understanding.

Area 7: Giving Praise

Do I use these guidelines to give positive attention?

➲ Make it strategic: praise those behaviors you want to see more often.

➲ Acknowledge good behavior immediately.

➲ Praise often, but make praise specific.

➲ Be genuine.

Area 8: Using Rewards

Do I use rewards and incentives such as those below, when positive attention is not enough?

➲ Use privileges and activities as rewards.

➲ Add individual, classwide, or group rewards.

➲ Use token economies with short- and long-term rewards.

➲ Have students pick their own rewards.

➲ Use reward menus; change rewards frequently.

➲ Set realistic goals.

➲ Have students self-monitor and evaluate their own behavior.

➲ Draw up a contract with the student.

Area 9: Giving Corrective Feedback

Do I use the prudent negative consequences defined below?

- ⮌ Catch problem behavior as soon as it starts.
- ⮌ Be very brief, using only a few words.
- ⮌ Stay calm and matter of fact.
- ⮌ Don't use more than one warning.
- ⮌ Give feedback privately to the student.
- ⮌ Use response cost, work tasks, or time-out.
- ⮌ Don't rely on negative consequences alone.

Area 10: Communication With Parents

Do I involve parents?

- ⮌ Contact parents early on.
- ⮌ Promote a team spirit.
- ⮌ Use a daily school-home report card with consequences at home.
- ⮌ Make homework expectations explicit.

PUTTING IT ALL TOGETHER: SAMPLE SOLUTIONS TO COMMON PROBLEMS OF STUDENTS WITH ADHD

You can use the strategies checklist below to handle eight common problems. Next to each problem are the numbers of the strategy areas on the above checklist that were used to solve the problem.

PROBLEM 1: STARTING AND STOPPING TASKS/ACTIVITIES ON TIME

Areas: 1, 2, 3, 4, 6, 7

Ryan, a fourth-grader, had great difficulty getting started on his assignments. He often couldn't seem to find the right page in the book or the materials he needed. Then, once started, he had trouble stopping when he was told to and switching to another activity.

Solution: Ryan's teacher decided to move his seat to the front where she could assist him during transitions. She made a point of making sure he understood the instructions by having him repeat them back to her. She praised him for accuracy. She also decided to use a check-off card that included the steps he needed to follow to start a task (get the right book, find the right page, get pencil and paper, do the first problem, or read the first paragraph). Ryan would check off each step as it was completed. The teacher praised him for using the card and getting started on his work. To help him stop activities, she gave him advance warning and clear, specific directions. She also gave extra praise for stopping when told to stop.

PROBLEM 2: DISRUPTIONS: CALLING OUT, INTERRUPTING, MAKING TOO MUCH NOISE

Areas: 1, 5, 7, 8, 9

Justin, a second-grader, was very loud and impulsive in class. He often blurted out during class discussions. He bothered his neighbors during independent seatwork by whispering or making noises.

Solution: Justin's teacher decided to move his seat away from peers who were likely to interact with him at the wrong times. He also established a class rule for hand-raising and posted it on the wall. Whenever he saw Justin following the rule, he praised him (as he did other children following the rule). These changes helped, but Justin continued to call out in class. So, his teacher decided to use a response cost/token program. The token was a card with three pictures of a raised hand. He gave Justin a "token" card for every period (there were six periods during the day). Every time he called out, the teacher crossed out a hand. At the end of the day, Justin counted the number of hands left on his card. For every hand left, he could earn one minute of time on the computer.

PROBLEM 3: NOT ATTENDING TO LECTURES AND CLASS DISCUSSIONS

Areas: 2, 7, 8

Scott, a fifth-grader, routinely daydreamed during class. His teacher noticed that even though he was seated near the front, he seemed to drift off into his own world. He seldom asked questions or participated in class discussions. The teacher was also concerned that the whole class was starting to tune out lectures.

Solution: Scott's teacher decided to change some things to improve the attention and participation of all the students. He began making discussions more interesting for everyone by using relevant examples and more hands-on activities. He frequently repeated what he said to make sure everyone heard. He prompted students to pay attention and participate by implementing a classwide reward program in which all students earned points for participating in class discussions and answering "attention checks" accurately. Attention checks involved asking students impromptu questions about the material being discussed. To make sure all students were called on, the teacher made up a deck of cards with each student's name on a card. He randomly pulled a card from the deck to determine who would be asked each attention check. Because Scott had particular difficulty attending, he made sure to call on Scott at a more frequent rate than the other students. Points were accumulated every day and earnings were publicly posted on a chart in the room. After the chart was filled up (this took several weeks), the class earned a popcorn party.

The teacher also did several things specifically to help Scott. He told Scott in advance that he would be called on during group lessons. He also increased his involvement in the lesson by having Scott keep track of participation points earned during discussions, using Scott's work as a sample for the whole class and having Scott demonstrate principles related to the lecture (with help as needed).

PROBLEM 4: NOT COMPLETING WORK

Areas: 3, 4, 7, 8, 10

Lisa, a third-grader, seldom completed assigned work. She seemed to understand the concepts, but it took great effort on her part to stay focused. She often became frustrated when she did not complete the work on time and would give up. She seemed to be losing interest in school.

Solution: Lisa's teacher took a two-pronged approach to the problem. First, she made accommodations to the assignments, and second, she set up a daily school-home contract with completed work as the target behavior. Lisa earned a point for all assignments completed accurately and neatly. She used a timer to help Lisa complete assignments more quickly. She set the timer at the beginning of independent seatwork. If Lisa "beat the clock" she was able to earn bonus points on her school-home contract. The teacher reduced the quantity of repetitive work but told Lisa that she could earn extra bonus points for completing more than the modified assignment. Lisa was also given extra time to complete her work. She exchanged her points for daily rewards (TV time) and weekly rewards (eating out) at home.

PROBLEM 5: DEFIANT, AGGRESSIVE BEHAVIOR

Areas: 5, 6, 7, 8, 9

David, a first-grader, was extremely defiant during class. He refused to follow teacher directions and made rude remarks under his breath. He teased his classmates and would push or hit them if they got in his way.

Solution: David's teacher decided to do several things. First, she clarified that a class rule prohibited hitting and saying mean things. She made sure to catch David when he was getting along with peers and following her directions. She praised him and reminded him that he was working toward being able to earn recess and free time because he was showing self-control. She also established time-out and work tasks as consequences for hitting or pushing. Whenever David was aggressive, he would get a 10-minute time-out in the back of the class. If he went right away, that amount was reduced to two minutes. If he didn't go to time-out, he also had to do ten tasks. Each task involved drawing a diagonal line through a small box. Tasks not completed during class were completed after school.

PROBLEM 6: NOT FOLLOWING DIRECTIONS

Areas: 6, 7, 8

Maya, a fourth-grader, often failed to follow teacher instructions to sit down, stop talking to her neighbor, put her book away, line up, and so on. She wasn't defiant; she simply didn't seem to hear the instruction or seemed to forget it right after she heard it. She was easily distracted by other things, which didn't help matters.

Solution: Maya's teacher decided to change the way she gave directions. She stopped giving directions by asking questions and made her directions very clear, brief, and specific, and only gave one at a time. She began having Maya repeat the direction to make sure she understood. She praised Maya when she followed directions right away. (She found that praising her as she started to comply often prompted her to finish complying!) Just changing the way she gave instructions seemed to help, but she decided to start a group reward program to help all students follow directions right away. She divided the class into six teams corresponding to the six rows of students. She gave out row points for those rows that followed directions right away. Row points were totaled every day. Rows with the most points earned privileges the next day (lining up first). Row points were also accumulated for a class party.

PROBLEM 7: LOW FRUSTRATION TOLERANCE

Areas: 6, 7, 8, 10

Mark, a second-grader, easily became upset whenever something did not go the way he wanted it to go. Any disappointment would trigger a tantrum.

Solution: Mark's teacher began a program to help Mark learn to tolerate disappointments. He told Mark that he was going to look for situations that often made Mark frustrated, such as getting called out in a game, not being chosen for an activity, having to wait to get help from the teacher when he was busy, and not being able to do a certain activity on a given day. When he saw that Mark was accepting a situation he didn't like without crying, complaining, or tantrumming, he praised Mark and gave him a point for accepting on his school-home report card. To help him out, the teacher would also try to prompt Mark with a direction to show accepting right before a potential disappointment.

PROBLEM 8: TRANSITION PROBLEMS

Area: 3

Erik, a sixth-grader, was very disorganized. He seldom retrieved or put away his books, pencils, paper, and other materials in a timely fashion, and he seemed to always be losing his things.

Solution: Erik's teacher assigned him a study buddy. The buddy was a classmate who was chosen because he was mild mannered and well organized. Before each period, the teacher would tell both boys to get the materials they needed together. At the end of each period, they would put their books and materials away together. The study buddy served as a model for how to handle materials and keep organized during transitions.

CHAPTER 7

EVALUATING WHETHER THE PROGRAM IS WORKING

How do you know if the program is working? The obvious answer is that the program is working if the problem behavior is decreased and some alternative acceptable behavior is in its place. Many teachers have a sense of this, but accurate, objective records of the child's behavior are necessary to know for sure. The best way to track progress is by keeping daily charts or logs of the student's performance. If a token system is used, this may simply be the number of tokens earned per day.

If behavior is improving and the program seems to be working, keep it up for at least two to three weeks without changing it. Then if success continues, you can begin to make modifications to expand the program, further shape behavior to your eventual goal, or even begin fading the program.

HOW TO AVOID SINKING YOUR OWN SHIP

If the program is not working, identify the reasons for its failure. Without realizing it, teachers are sometimes their own worst enemies in the classroom. Many of the approaches recommended here can be rendered ineffective by common teaching mistakes. When this happens, the teacher may be incorrectly convinced that the techniques don't work and then may abandon tools that could have helped him or her be more successful in teaching. A list of suggestions follows that will keep you from undermining your effectiveness.

HOW TO HAVE AN EFFECTIVE PROGRAM

1. Don't argue back. DO NOT let yourself be drawn into an argument or discussion of your rules or whether the student was following them. State the facts and give your interventions without responding to protests.

2. Don't give unnecessary explanations. In most cases, it is unnecessary to provide a rationale for your commands or rules. Giving rationales often only invites arguments or causes the student to focus on the rationale rather than on the command.

3. Don't yell. It is often more effective to lower your voice when redirecting a student. Displays of emotion (anger, exasperation) can be rewarding for many students.

4. Don't take good behavior for granted.

5. Don't follow rewards with a negative comment (e.g., "Why can't you do this all the time?").

6. Don't give half-hearted praise in a tone suggesting that you don't mean it.

7. Don't criticize or humiliate the student in front of the class.

8. Don't give in and let the student have the reward before he or she has earned it.

9. Don't give in and let the student have the reward when they plead or throw tantrums.

10. Don't give too many second chances.

11. Don't forget about the program or forget to complete the daily report card.

12. Don't expect too much or set the standards for reward too high for an individual ADHD student.

13. Don't expect too little.

14. Don't give up once the student loses interest in the reward. Know in advance that your reward program will work for a while and then lose its effectiveness. Modify the program, but do not abandon it.

COMMON REASONS FOR PROGRAM FAILURE

1. Target behavior is vague ("Be a good student.")

2. Consequences are not immediate enough. (Only a weekly reward is given.)

3. Student was never interested in the reward or lost interest in it. (Not all kids like candy, for example.)

4. Student does not mind the negative consequence. (Some students don't like recess anyway.)

5. Peers are reinforcing the negative behavior. (Getting a classmate to laugh at silly behavior is a powerful reinforcer.)

6. Other factors reinforce the negative behavior. (A student throws a tantrum in class and gets out of doing the work.)

7. The program is not practical to do. (There are too many target behaviors, or they're too complicated.)

8. Parents undermine the program. (Parents don't agree with the teacher's concerns.)

9. Parents don't follow through with home consequences. (Parents are too busy to give rewards at home.)

10. Program is not clear to the student. (Student can't describe her own program accurately.)

APPLY PROBLEM SOLVING TO MODIFY THE PROGRAM

Follow these steps to help you identify some possible solutions and evaluate whether they will solve the problem.

➦ First, make a list of some reasons why the program may not be working.

➦ Next, brainstorm some solutions.

➦ Then, select those solutions most likely to help the problem.

➦ Implement the changes and evaluate. Did the changes fix the problem? If not, are there other solutions to try?

Remember: Most programs will require some modification initially and over time to be successful. The need for change does not mean behavioral programs are not effective. It is simply part of what makes them work.

Example 1: Remember Maya in the example on page 147? She had trouble following directions promptly. At first, she responded well to the teacher changing the way she gave commands and the row points. But after a few weeks, Maya began not following directions again.

First, make a list of some reasons why the program may not be working:

- ⮐ Maya lost interest in the reward of a class party.

- ⮐ The reward may be too far in the future.

- ⮐ I've stopped having her repeat the direction after I give it.

Next, brainstorm some solutions:

- ⮐ Change the group reward.

- ⮐ Use an individual reward in addition to the group reward.

- ⮐ Make the reward more immediate.

- ⮐ Continue having Maya repeat the direction.

Then, select those solutions most likely to help the problem:

- ⮐ Add an individual daily reward for Maya on days she follows most directions right away. The reward will be given by Maya's parents at home through use of a daily report card.

- ⮐ Have her repeat the directions again.

- ⮐ Implement the changes and evaluate. Did the changes fix the problem? If not, are there other solutions to try?

- ⮐ Maya started following directions again. I'll plan to reevaluate the program in two weeks to see if additional changes are needed.

Example 2: David, the defiant and aggressive student describes on page 147, did not seem to be responding to the punishment of time-out and work tasks. He was receiving five to six time-outs per day.

First, make a list of some reasons why the program may not be working:

- ⮐ I'm not staying very calm when he defies me, and he seems to be successful at getting me to argue with him about his behavior.

- ⮐ I might be giving him too many warnings before sending him to time-out.

⊃ These problems may be making time-out less of a punishment.

⊃ The praise I'm giving may not be a powerful enough reinforcer.

Next, brainstorm some solutions:

⊃ Stay calm and avoid arguments at all cost!

⊃ Have David go to time-out right away. No second chances.

⊃ Give him lots of praise when he follows my directions.

⊃ Let him earn stickers if he doesn't have more than one time-out a day.

Then, select those solutions most likely to help the problem:

⊃ All of the above

⊃ Implement changes and evaluate:

⊃ It worked! David stopped being so defiant and seemed to like earning the stickers.

Example 3: Fabiano & Pelham (2003) describe the following case study to illustrate how modifications to an existing behavior management plan can be key to its success. They report that John, a third-grader, showed high levels of disruptive behavior and low levels of on-task behavior. The teacher had been using a daily behavior sheet targeting five posted rules: finish work, follow directions, work quietly, cooperate with peers and adults, and stay on task. After each activity, John and his teacher discussed whether he had met each goal. If they decided he had, he colored in a square on a graph paper. Once he colored in a predetermined number of squares he could earn a reward (trading cards). This would take about two weeks. However, he had not earned the reward after this program had been in place for more than three weeks. He was continuing to get out of his seat, tease peers, call out, not comply, and not complete his work. The teacher was concerned that "nothing motivated him." Three changes were made to John's program: 1) He was given the opportunity to earn daily rewards (access to a hand-held computer game for meeting goals in the morning and then again for meeting goals in the afternoon). 2) Teachers provided immediate feedback whenever he exhibited negative behavior rather than waiting until the end of the period (to which he responded well). 3) Behavior criteria on the goal sheet were operationalized as less than three violations of each rule rather than being based on student-teacher consensus. Dramatic reduction in disruptive behavior and increase in on-task behavior resulted from these minor adjustments to the behavior program.

CHAPTER 8

ADHD BEYOND THE CLASSROOM

HOW IS ADD/ADHD IDENTIFIED?

ADHD is not an easy disorder to diagnose. All of the symptoms are characteristic of normal childhood, so it becomes critical to discriminate between the disorder and normal child development. It is equally important to discriminate ADHD from other disorders since symptoms of other disorders can often look like ADHD. Because of the diagnostic complications, it is imperative that the diagnostic evaluation be conducted by a professional well trained in psychiatric diagnoses, child psychopathology, normal child development, and psychometrics. Usually a clinical psychologist, child psychiatrist, or behavioral pediatrician with expertise in ADD/ADHD, disruptive behavior, and emotional problems has the training and background to provide a diagnostic evaluation. There is also a growing trend to provide school psychologists with the skills needed for assessing ADHD.

THE DIAGNOSTIC CRITERIA FOR ADHD

The psychiatric diagnosis of ADHD is made using the criteria outlined in *Diagnostic and Statistical Manual for Mental Disorders* (*DSM-IV*). To meet the criteria for ADHD, at least six of the symptoms in one of the following two groupings must have been present for at least six months to a degree that is maladaptive and inconsistent with developmental level.

PROBLEMS WITH INATTENTION

The student often:

- fails to give close attention to details or makes careless mistakes in schoolwork, work, or other activities

- has difficulty sustaining attention in tasks or play activities

- does not seem to listen when spoken to directly

- does not follow through on instructions and fails to finish schoolwork, chores, or duties in the workplace

- has difficulty organizing tasks and activities

- avoids, dislikes, or is reluctant to engage in tasks that require sustained mental effort (such as schoolwork or homework)

- loses things necessary for tasks or activities (e.g., toys, school assignments, pencils, books, or tools)

- is easily distracted by extraneous stimuli

- is often forgetful in daily activities

PROBLEMS WITH HYPERACTIVITY OR IMPULSIVITY

The student often:

- fidgets with hands or feet and squirms in seat

- leaves seat in classroom or in other situations in which remaining seated is expected

- runs about or climbs excessively in situations in which it is inappropriate

- has difficulty playing or engaging in leisure activities quietly

- is "on the go" or often acts as if "driven by a motor"

- talks excessively

- blurts out answers before questions have been completed

- has difficulty awaiting turn

- interrupts or intrudes on others

In addition, the symptoms need to have been present since before the child turned 7 years old and must cause social or academic impairment in at least two settings (e.g., at home and school).

SUBTYPES OF ADHD

ADHD-Predominantly Inattentive Type: High on inattention (six or more from the list of nine inattention symptoms) and low on hyperactive-impulsive (less than six hyperactive-impulsive symptoms).

ADHD-Predominantly Hyperactive-Impulsive Type: Low on inattention (less than six inattention symptoms) and high on hyperactive-impulsive (six or more hyperactive-impulsive symptoms).

ADHD-Combined Type: High on inattention (six or more inattention symptoms) and high on hyperactive-impulsive (six or more hyperactive-impulsive symptoms).

Note that the *DSM* criteria for ADHD are currently being evaluated, and changes to reflect new scientific understanding of ADHD are expected for the fifth version of the *DSM* (expected publication date: 2013). For example, the specific symptoms and cut-offs might be adjusted for gender and age (e.g., so that more symptoms are required for preschoolers than adolescents). In addition, the age of onset may be increased since the requirement of onset prior to age 7 excludes cases having serious impairment but which do not become noticeable until older childhood. This may be particularly relevant for ADHD-Inattentive Type.

Diagnostic methods: State-of-the-art methods for assessing ADHD include review of birth, developmental and medical history, review of school records, completion of standardized rating scales by parents and teachers, symptom-related interviews administered to parents and teachers (if possible), review of social and emotional functioning, and intelligence and achievement testing to assess for learning problems.

Note about other diagnostic methods: Sometimes practitioners will recommend other diagnostic tests such as brain scans, computer tests, and so on. These do not have supporting scientific data for use as valid indicators of ADHD and are not needed to make a diagnosis.

WHAT SHOULD YOU DO IF YOU SUSPECT A STUDENT MAY HAVE ADHD?

As a teacher, you may be one of the first to notice a child's extreme inattention, impulsivity, or overactivity in a structured setting. Parents have often observed difficulty at home, but in many cases, problems are more obvious in school.

As a first step, collect information regarding the student's academic work and behavior in class. Be specific about your concerns; this information will be useful in communicating with parents and other school personnel.

Next, consult with or make a referral to the school psychologist, guidance counselor, special education teacher, principal, or other school personnel with expertise in ADHD or attention/behavior problems. Have a specialist in handling these problems informally observe the student in your class. A referral for a formal assessment may be needed to evaluate ADHD-related concerns. If so, you should be aware of your school's policy for making referrals to evaluate the need for special services. There are several mechanisms to obtain services for students with ADHD (see page 160), and very specific legal guidelines usually need to be followed. Remember that the diagnosis of ADHD requires special training and experience and will need to be made by a professional who specializes in assessing and treating ADHD.

You don't need to wait for the results of the evaluation to begin implementing interventions in the classroom. Share your concerns about specific problems with the parents. You may wish to start a school-home intervention or make additional accommodations for the student in class immediately. Keep records of the student's response to these interventions, including all work samples and behavior records. These records are important for gauging the student's progress and determining the need for additional intervention. They will also be helpful in the event that a student study team meeting takes place.

REMEMBER THAT THE DIAGNOSIS OF ADHD REQUIRES SPECIAL TRAINING AND EXPERIENCE AND WILL NEED TO BE MADE BY A PROFESSIONAL WHO SPECIALIZES IN ASSESSING AND TREATING ADHD.

■ ■ ■

WHAT ARE THE ROLES OF PROFESSIONALS IN MAKING A DIAGNOSIS AND PROVIDING TREATMENT?

A number of different professionals are usually involved in evaluating and treating ADHD. School personnel, psychologists, physicians, outside professionals, and parents need to work together as part of a team. Clear communication among everyone is essential.

Teacher's role: As a part of the evaluation, you will likely be called upon to give a detailed description of the student's academic progress, behavior, and social relations in class and to complete a series of standard behavior rating scales. Your input to the diagnostic process is critical. School is very often the place in which children have the most difficulty. You are in the best position to provide information about the child's behavior at school. Take the time to be accurate. In addition to providing information for the evaluation, don't be hesitant about asking questions of the team. Get their ideas for working with the ADHD child in class.

Role of psychologist: A clinical psychologist with expertise in working with ADHD can provide the evaluation. The psychologist often serves as the case coordinator, gathering information from all sources, and integrating the data to formulate diagnostic impressions and make recommendations. The psychologist usually interviews the parents to assess the child's development, history of problems, and current symptoms. The psychologist also interviews the teacher (if possible) and child. Psychologists interpret behavior rating scales and checklists completed by parents and teachers and review school records. Psychologists also administer intelligence and achievement tests (supplemented with neuropsychological tests, if necessary) to evaluate for possible learning disabilities. At the end of the evaluation, diagnostic impressions are provided by the psychologist, usually in the form of a written report, and recommendations for further evaluation or treatment are made. Psychologists may provide treatments such as parent training, family therapy, and social skills training. They may also consult with teachers and parents about setting up coordinated school-home programs.

Role of physician: A child psychiatrist or behavioral pediatrician can also provide an evaluation for ADHD. The physician performs a medical and developmental history and obtains information from parents and children about current functioning and symptoms. They complete physical and neurological exams to assess for medical problems that may accompany ADHD; however, these exams are not necessary for a diagnosis of ADHD. Physicians may also use standardized parent and teacher ratings of behavior. Unlike psychologists, physicians do not usually administer cognitive tests such as IQ and achievement tests. Physicians provide recommendations for treatment following the evaluation. Physicians often recommend the use of medication to treat ADHD. Physicians, but not psychologists, can prescribe medication.

Role of school psychologist: School psychologists with expertise in ADHD may provide many of the same procedures as a clinical psychologist. An advantage they have is the ability to observe the child directly during class. This is usually impractical for an outside professional to do. The school psychologist plays a key role in facilitating the initial evaluation and setting up a student study meeting where all school personnel, outside professionals, and the child's parents can meet about the student's educational needs, the possibility of special education, and setting up necessary interventions for the student at school. Many school psychologists also have training in working with students with ADHD in class and can make recommendations for accommodations and management plans in the classroom.

Role of school social worker: Social workers provide counseling and related support services for children at school. They do not usually perform formal evaluations or psychological testing. However, they do usually attend SSTs and IEPs. Some may assist teachers in making recommendations for accommodations and management plans for the classroom.

Role of school administration: The role of the administrative staff is one of setting the stage so that quality education can happen. Effective administrators encourage training in methods for working with students with ADHD and provide opportunities for in-services on ADHD. They know that working with students with ADHD can be extremely challenging and demoralizing for any teacher. They do their best to provide necessary support staff, materials, and supplies and they attend student study-team meetings. They recognize the efforts of their teachers and routinely offer support.

THE ROLE OF THE ADMINISTRATIVE STAFF IS ONE OF SETTING THE STAGE SO THAT QUALITY EDUCATION CAN HAPPEN.

■ ■ ■

EDUCATIONAL IDENTIFICATION AND POLICIES RELEVANT FOR ADHD

THE NEED FOR SPECIAL EDUCATION SERVICES REQUIRES DOCUMENTATION OF ACADEMIC IMPAIRMENT IN ADDITION TO A DIAGNOSIS OF ADHD.

■ ■ ■

During recent years, educational policy regarding ADHD has been at the forefront of debate at the federal, state, and district level. As more is known of the disorder, as more organized parent advocacy groups have formed, and as more educators have become familiar with the range of handicaps these children exhibit in class, policy has been clarified and shaped to offer more services to meet the needs of these children than ever before. At this time, two mechanisms exist for ADHD children to qualify for special services. These two mechanisms include the "Other Health Impaired" category of Part B of the Individuals with Disabilities Education Act (IDEA), which is an educational benefits law; and Section 504 of the Rehabilitation Act of 1973, which is a civil rights law. The U.S. Department of Education has indicated that both of these policies dictate that individuals with an attention deficit disorder that causes impairment in educational performance or substantial limitations in learning or behavior are eligible for services. Students may qualify for special education services under IDEA, and services are provided in accordance with an Individualized Education Program designed to meet the unique needs of the student. Section 504 ensures that individuals with disabilities have equal access to education as those who do not. Accommodations and modifications are made to the educational program to meet the unique needs of the qualifying student. Services provided under both mechanisms may include accommodations in the regular classroom, a resource program for part of the day, or a full-day, self-contained special education classroom.

School policy regarding methods for identifying ADHD and methods for documenting the need for special services may differ somewhat across districts. Historically, the diagnosis of ADHD has usually been farmed out to physicians and psychologists in the community, although some school psychologists with expertise in ADHD and training in diagnostic and assessment methods may provide the diagnosis. The need for special education services requires documentation of academic impairment in addition to a diagnosis of ADHD. Achievement tests are usually not sensitive for picking up such impairment. Instead, failure to complete assigned work (with accuracy) on a regular basis, or school records showing impaired study skills, disorganization, or other academic problems may be used to assess impairment. Not all students with ADHD will qualify for special services, since some may not be exhibiting educational impairment. For those who do qualify, the type of services should be tailored to the severity of the problems. Many students with ADHD will perform quite well with accommodations in the regular classroom; others with severe difficulties may require placement in more restrictive settings.

WHAT ARE THE EVIDENCE-BASED TREATMENTS FOR ADHD?

Evidence-based treatments are those that have been shown to be effective in well-controlled scientific studies, meaning that significantly greater improvement occurs among those receiving the treatment compared to those who do not or who receive some other form of treatment. The focus of this book has been on the evidence-based treatment most important for educators: classroom accommodations and behavior management strategies. Numerous research studies document positive effects from these strategies, and they are recommended for virtually all students with ADHD. Additional evidence-based treatments, however, are usually necessary to obtain the most successful outcomes. These include behavioral interventions for parents and families, skills training, and medication. Although no known treatment cures ADHD, behavioral interventions (in school and at home), often in combination with medication, can lead to dramatic improvement in overall functioning.

BEHAVIORAL INTERVENTIONS AT HOME

In reaction to the child's challenging behaviors, parenting practices are often more negative, inconsistent, and coercive, and also less positive and warm than in other families. Parents of children with ADHD are often very discouraged and lack confidence in their ability to parent effectively. It is crucial that parents receive help in how to manage their children's attention and behavior. Parent training or behavioral family therapy are the treatments of choice to address ADHD-related difficulties at home. In these approaches, parents are coached in how to use many of the same kinds of practices discussed for the classroom. They are taught how to improve the quality of their relationship with their child, and skills such as the use of praise and positive reinforcement, token economies, how to give effective commands and discipline, and how to establish effective routines for daily activities (getting ready in the morning, homework, evening activities). These interventions usually last for about 6–12 weeks. Research studies have shown them to be effective for families with children who have ADHD.

CHILD SKILLS INTERVENTIONS

Social skills training can assist in improving peer-related problems; a model for providing such training is provided in Chapter 2. This training is most useful when conducted in a group setting with other children and when integrated with parent and teacher strategies for generalizing the skills outside of the group, as is done in the Child Life and Attention Skills and Collaborative Life skills programs described at the end of Chapter 5 (Pfiffner et al., 2007). The Summer Treatment Program for ADHD is another intervention which includes strategies focused on improving peer relations and which shows positive outcomes in research studies (Waschbusch et al., 2008). While studies do support the utility of providing training for improving peer relations, it is imperative that skills taught during group lessons are reinforced outside of the group. Children usually will not transfer the skills on their own without the support of adults at school and at home. This means that child therapy groups for social skills in which parents and/or teachers are not directly involved to prompt and reinforce the skills outside of the group may not yield much benefit.

Educational therapy: Children with ADHD often have co-morbid learning disabilities. Although educational therapy is not considered a treatment for ADHD per se, it is the treatment of choice for those with learning disabilities. In addition, many educational therapists also provide interventions for improving organizational and study skills.

MEDICATION TREATMENTS

Medication therapy has been used to treat ADHD for over 60 years, and extensive research exists to support its efficacy and safety. Psychostimulant medications are the most widely used for treating ADHD—an estimated three to four percent of children in the U.S., or between 1.5 and 2.5 million children, take stimulant medication. These originally included only short-acting medicines (lasting three or four hours) such as Ritalin (methylphenidate) and Dexedrine (dextroamphetamine), which meant children often needed to take another dose of the medication while at school. In the past decade, longer-acting, sustained-release delivery systems have become the most popular, owing to the fact that these medicines allow for single dosages lasting 8 to 12 hours (so repeated doses of medicine during school hours are not required). Longer-acting forms of methylphenidate include Concerta, Ritalin LA, Focalin XR, Metadate CD, Daytrana transdermal system. Longer acting forms of amphetamine include Adderall XR and Vyvanse. As many as 70 to 80 percent of children and adolescents with ADHD respond positively to stimulant medication (Barkley, 2006). This usually means that when they take the medication they are able to focus their attention for longer periods of time, are less active and impulsive, are more compliant, get more of their work done, and get along better with others (teachers, parents, and other children). Non-stimulant medications including Strattera (atomoxetine) and Intuniv (guanfacine) also show positive effects in children with ADHD. Studies generally show that all subtypes of ADHD respond to medication, although the most obvious effects are for those having attention problems along with hyperactivity and impulsivity. Positive effects are limited to the time period in which the medication is taken. Medication does not cure ADHD; long-term effects and effects during non-medicated hours are not typically found.

Psychostimulant medication is thought to work by increasing activity and modulating arousal in the parts of the brain that control attention, inhibition, and activity level. However, the mechanism(s) accounting for the clinical effects are not clearly understood. Some people used to think that the medication had a paradoxical effect on ADHD children. But research studies show that stimulant medication seems to work the same way with both normal and ADHD children.

It is hard to predict who will respond well to medication and to what type and at what dose. This needs to be determined for each child. A consultation with a physician is required, and a medication trial is often done. The trial usually involves carefully monitoring a child's response to various dosages to determine the optimal level.

WHAT IS THE TEACHER'S ROLE IN MEDICATION TREATMENT?

Medication is prescribed mostly for school-related problems. Therefore, your role in communicating with parents and physicians is a critical one. First of all, teachers should provide information to the student's parents and physician about the student's behavioral, social, and academic performance in school prior to medication use. This kind of information is important as baseline data. It will be the standard against which the effects of medication will be measured.

After the child begins medication, you will be in the position to monitor the effects. Be prepared to provide feedback about the student's progress to the parents and physician. Some districts have standard reporting formats to use such as rating scales and questionnaires. You should look for possible positive changes in the child's behavior such as increased attention span and compliance, decreased impulsivity and physical activity, and increased work productivity. You should also look for possible negative effects. Some children show improved behavior but become over-focused and glassy-eyed on medication. Often this means that the dose is too high. Side effects are also common. These might include insomnia, appetite suppression, headaches, stomachaches, or increased motor or verbal tics. Some children also have mood swings or greater irritability, especially when the medication is wearing off. This information is important for the physician in determining the appropriateness of medication and the optimal type and dose.

After the best dose has been determined, keep monitoring the child. Communicate any changes in behavior or performance to the parents and physician. Sometimes adjustments in the type or dose of medication are necessary after a period of time.

Keep in mind that medication is only one tool for improving students' performance. Medication is not recommended as the sole treatment for ADHD. Other treatments such as classroom interventions and parent training are usually necessary.

ALTERNATIVE TREATMENTS

Alternative treatments are treatments that have too little scientific support to be considered empirically supported. In other words, if studies of the treatment have been conducted, they do not have adequate controls to allow for clear conclusions about the treatment's effects, they have not been published in scientifically reputable peer-reviewed sources, or the effects are not as strong as behavioral or medication treatments. Two alternative treatments (computer-based interventions and neurofeedback) show some preliminary positive effects as described below.

Computer-based interventions: Recent efforts have been made to attempt to train better attention and working memory using computer training. Special software programs have been developed to provide the training, such as Pay Attention!, BrainTrain, and Cogmed. Children complete a series of exercises on the computer that have a video game format and colorful graphics to capture their interest. The intensity of the training varies from 20 to 30 hours over the course of weeks or months. Initial outcomes show very modest positive effects, and mostly on analog tasks rather than children's attention during school. However, research is likely to continue to determine whether modifications to existing cognitive training interventions may yield more improvement.

Neurofeedback: Children with ADHD have been shown to have low levels of arousal in the frontal areas of the brain due to excess levels of slow waves (theta) and a deficit of fast waves (beta). This treatment trains children to increase arousal and thereby decrease symptoms of ADHD. The training involves connecting the child to a machine by placing electrodes on a child's head to monitor his or her own brain wave patterns. The child is given feedback (e.g., a tone, a visual cue in a video game) when the brain waves are of the desired frequency. The child's task is to learn to keep the wave patterns in the frontal areas of the brain at a high level. Positive effects of this treatment on ADHD symptoms have been found in a number of case studies. However, this treatment has not yet shown effects in rigorous scientific studies with the necessary controls in place to assess its actual efficacy.

Other alternative treatments: A number of other treatments have been touted as being effective with ADHD children, but insufficient research data supports their use. These include megavitamins, nutritional supplements, chiropractics, and vision therapy. At this time, these treatments are not evidence-based. It is also important to note that individual therapies (e.g., play therapy, "talk" therapy) may be useful for dealing with emotional problems but are not effective for treating ADHD.

A NUMBER OF OTHER TREATMENTS HAVE BEEN TOUTED AS BEING EFFECTIVE WITH ADHD CHILDREN, BUT INSUFFICIENT RESEARCH DATA SUPPORTS THEIR USE.

■ ■ ■

CHAPTER 9

THE EFFECTS OF ADHD ON TEACHERS

The secondary demoralization often found in children with ADHD can also be found among their teachers! As most of you who have worked with an ADHD student know, it is demanding and may continually challenge your sense of competence as a teacher. The high rate of movement, interruptions, disruption, and talkativeness can be difficult to tolerate over time. You may find yourself giving the ADHD student more commands and directions. When met with resistance, you may find yourself escalating in response. Feelings of frustration, anger, and hostility are not unusual. You may feel that you have exhausted your resources and are not sure where to turn.

One of the most important things to remember is: Don't take it personally! Students with ADHD are challenging even to the most seasoned teacher. They are often unaware of their most disturbing behaviors, and when they are aware, they often can't seem to stop themselves. Another important point: Don't fall into the trap of thinking that students with ADHD can behave as well as other students if they only try harder. ADHD is not an intentional problem. However, with the right tools and techniques these students *can* be successful, and you can begin to enjoy their unique strengths.

Many teachers who have worked with students with ADHD for years and routinely use strategies discussed in this book actually prefer teaching these students over their "normal" counterparts. They like the sense of challenge and the sense of reward. Invariably, they report that these students have forced them to improve their teaching skills.

There are many teacher characteristics that seem to be important when working with students with ADHD. Teachers who seem to do well and enjoy working with students with ADHD tend to be patient, flexible, knowledgeable about intervention strategies and open-minded about learning new ones, enjoy collaborating with a multidisciplinary team, and have a positive attitude about children with special needs. They often have high energy themselves and a strong interest in and commitment to teaching.

ENERGIZING AND REENERGIZING FOR TEACHERS

Below are some suggestions for keeping up your energy for teaching:

1. Being around students with ADHD can be exhausting. Implementing a consistent behavior modification program with students with ADHD is a tough job. Don't neglect your own emotional needs. Don't count on the students to meet all of your needs. Make sure you have outlets for reenergizing: Exercise regularly, talk to friends, consult with colleagues, take a break before you see your own kids, and so on. Remember to get plenty of sleep and don't lose your sense of humor!

2. Set small goals for yourself and reward yourself every step of the way. Take one day at a time. Treat yourself for remembering to catch good behavior or staying calm during an outburst. Give yourself a special treat for taking the extra time needed to be consistent.

3. Get help from other professionals. No one has all the answers. Sometimes it's easier for a person not so involved in the situation to look at the student objectively. Set up a support system with other teachers to help keep you motivated and consistent. Give each other daily support for following through and coping with difficult behaviors. Surround yourself with positive teachers, not complainers!

4. Expect that you will have "bad" days. You may find that you have slipped out of the habits of good behavior management. Encourage yourself not give up. Don't let yourself get trapped by feelings of guilt or inadequacy. It's okay to make mistakes.

5. Expect setbacks. Students may inexplicably "blow it" after you have invested a great deal of yourself in their progress. Sometimes these setbacks can be resolved by your staying steadfastly consistent with the program you have established; other times you may need to modify the program. In either case, consider these setbacks as part of the ADHD student's training and learn to separate yourself from them.

6. Don't give up! Behavior can change slowly, and the benefits of your efforts may not be seen immediately. Your belief in your students will be felt and will make a difference in their lives.

CHAPTER 10

QUESTIONS AND ANSWERS

Is there a "test" for ADHD?

At present, there are no definitive biological tests (e.g., blood tests, brain scans, X-rays) or cognitive tests (e.g., continuous performance tests, computerized tests of learning, IQ tests, achievement tests) that can validly diagnose ADHD. In addition, it is inappropriate to base a diagnosis of ADHD solely on the child's behavior during a one-time visit to a physician or psychologist. Instead, accurate diagnosis requires a comprehensive medical and developmental history, interviews and behavior ratings from parents, teachers, and other significant adults in the child's life, review of specific problem areas and symptoms, school records, academic performance measures, and observation of the child's behavior.

Isn't it unfair to reward students with ADHD for things that other students do automatically?

Many teachers struggle with this idea. Some believe providing high rates of praise and other rewards is unfair unless all students are rewarded the same way or that providing such rewards is tantamount to reinforcing the problem. Others say that adding reward programs to their classroom takes too much time away from teaching. Still others believe that students should learn through intrinsic or natural rewards such as the excitement in learning new things, getting good grades, or making new friends.

Unfortunately, students with ADHD do not usually respond to the typical consequences that work for other students. Many of the rewards in classrooms are too delayed, too weak, or not stimulating enough to motivate an ADHD student. Ordinary reinforcers, such as a teacher's approval or the satisfaction of a job well done, do not stop these children from getting in trouble even though they know what they are doing is wrong. They are driven by the moment to seek what's stimulating and interesting. This is part of their biological make-up.

To help students with ADHD learn to regulate their behavior, block out distractions, and focus on the task at hand, they need frequent, high-interest, salient rewards for meeting specific goals. If you are concerned that this practice is unfair, you may be equating fairness with treating all students the same way. Fairness in an educational sense is probably better defined as treating each student in a manner that affords success for that student (Gordon & Asher, 1994). For the ADHD student, more intense rewards are often what's required.

How do I find the time to praise?

With practice, praise takes only a few seconds. Decide on the behaviors you want to praise ahead of time. Then decide on the number of times you want to give praise each period. Use a counter or tally to keep track. Post stickers that remind you to praise. If you are spending lots of time attending to negative behavior, you'll find that as you praise more, you probably won't have to spend so much time reprimanding.

What do I do if another student complains because the ADHD student is getting rewards?

If you use individual reward programs, they should be set up privately between you and the child. Using home-based rewards rather than rewards at school helps keep the program private. If other children ask about it, tell them it's something only between you and the child. Most kids understand why the child is being treated differently and also realize the benefits to the class for that child getting along better with peers. Students who are very upset about another student having a reward program are often the ones who would benefit from a program, too. Some teachers prefer to use classwide programs to minimize this problem.

These strategies sound like too much external control. Don't we want to teach self-control?

The first step to teaching self-control is to teach kids to respond to external rules and contingencies. As kids are successful in following these rules, they can gradually be taught methods for inhibiting their own impulses and developing better self-control. However, expect that some external contingencies will always be necessary.

Won't reducing assignments just lead to academic problems or more behavior problems in the future?

Academic problems can result if reducing assignments means the students don't learn the material. To avoid this possibility, make sure you only reduce assignments for those students who already understand the concepts but who have trouble finishing lengthy assignments. The recommended focus here is on quality, not quantity, of work. Assignment reductions are probably most appropriate for students whose inattention and impulsivity are interfering with their ability to complete work. Work reduced for students who are willfully refusing to complete it may reinforce their negative behavior. Remember that these accommodations are meant to provide a mechanism for meeting the special needs of ADHD children and to promote success, enhanced self-esteem, and continued interest in school. If they are not serving that purpose, other interventions should be tried.

What do I do if my token reward system works initially, then stops working?

This common problem often occurs because the student has lost interest in the rewards or may be "testing the system." In any case, don't be fooled into thinking that reward systems are ineffective. The target behavior may need to be defined more clearly, the criteria for earning rewards may need to be lowered, consequences may need to be made more consistent or immediate, or alternatively, more powerful rewards may need to be used. These kinds of adjustments are to be expected.

Should we reduce our expectations of students with ADHD or excuse their behavior or academic underproductivity because they are unable to do better?

Helping the ADHD child does not mean taking away his or her responsibility to follow rules of behavior, comply with teacher directions, and complete assigned work. However, it does mean helping the child overcome his or her deficits and obstacles to doing these expected activities. This help includes increased structure, salience, clarity, and repetition. It also includes increased incentives for following rules and task completion, negative consequences for violations, and decreased expectations of completing assigned work independently without benefit of structure and incentives. Put the structure and incentives in place. Then let the child be responsible for his or her behavior.

REFERENCES AND READINGS

Abikoff, H., & Gallagher, R. (2008). Assessment and remediation of organizational skills deficits in children with ADHD. In K. McBurnett and L. J. Pfiffner (Eds.), *Attention deficit hyperactivity disorder: Concepts, controversies, new directions.* New York: Informa Healthcare.

Agler, D. (1995). Using the goodsport thermometer. Unpublished manuscript.

American Psychiatric Association. (1994). *Diagnostic and statistical manual of mental disorders* (4th ed.). Washington, DC: American Psychiatric Association.

Barkley, R. A. (2006). *Attention-deficit hyperactivity disorder: A handbook for diagnosis and treatment* (3rd ed.). New York: Guilford Press.

Barkley, R. A., Shelton, T. L., Crosswait, C., Moorehouse, M., Fletcher, K., Barrett, S., Jenkins, L., & Metevia, L. (2009). Multi-method psycho-educational intervention for preschool children with disruptive behavior: Preliminary results at post-treatment. *Journal of Child Psychology and Psychiatry, 41,* 319–332.

Barrish, H. H., Saunders, M., & Wold, M. M. (1969). The Good Behavior Game. Retrieved March, 2010 from http://www.interventioncentral.org/index.php/behavorial-resources.

Cunningham, C. E., Cunningham, L. J., & Martorelli, V. (2001). *Coping with conflict at school: The Collaborative Student Mediation Project manual.* Hamilton, Ontario, Canada: COPE Works.

Daly, P. M., & Ranalli, P. (2003). Using countoons to teach self-monitoring skills. *Teaching Exceptional Children, 35*(5), 30–35.

Davies, W., & Witte, R. (2000). Self-management and peer-monitoring within a group contingency to decrease uncontrolled verbalizations of children with ADHD. *Psychology in the Schools, 37*(2), 135–147.

DuPaul, G. J., & Stoner, G. (2003). ADHD in the schools: Assessment and intervention strategies (2nd ed.). New York: Guilford Press.

Dweck, C. S. (2006). *Mindset: The new psychology of success.* New York: Random House.

Evans, S. W., Langberg, J., Raggi, V., Allen, J., & Buvinger, E. C. (2005). Development of a school-based treatment program for middle school youth with ADHD. *Journal of Attention Disorders, 9*(1), 343–353.

Fabiano, G. A., & Pelham, W. E. (2003). Improving the effectiveness of behavioral classroom interventions for attention-deficit/hyperactivity disorder: A case study. *Journal of Emotional and Behavioral Disorders, 11*(2), 122–128.

Fabiano, G. A., Pelham, W. E., Coles, E. K., Gnagy, E. M., Chronis-Tuscano, A., & O'Connor, B. C. (2009). A meta-analysis of behavioral treatments for attention-deficit/hyperactivity disorder. *Clinical Psychology Review, 29,* 129–140.

Fabiano, G. A., Pelham, W. E., Gnagy, E. M., Burrows-MacLean, L., Coles, E. K., Chacko, A., et al. (2007). The single and combined effects of multiple intensities of behavior modification and multiple intensities of methylphenidate in a classroom setting. *School Psychology Review, 36,* 195–216.

Fabiano, G. A., Pelham, W. E., Karmazin, K., Kreher, J., Panahon, C. J., & Carlson, C. (2008). A group contingency program to improve the behavior of elementary school students in a cafeteria. *Behavior Modification, 32,* 121–132.

Fabiano, G. A., Pelham, W. E., Manos, M. J., Gnagy, E. M., Chronis, A. M., Onyango, A. N. et al. (2004). An evaluation of three time-out procedures for children with attention-deficit/hyperactivity disorder. *Behavior Therapy, 35,* 449–469.

Fabiano, G. A., Vujnovic, R. K., Pelham, W. E., Waschbusch, D. A., Massetti, G. M., Pariseau, M. E. et al. (2010). Enhancing the effectiveness of special education programming for children with attention deficit hyperactivity disorder using a daily report card. *School Psychology Review, 39*(2), 219–239.

Fine, A. H., & Kotkin, R. A. (Eds.). (2003). *Therapist's guide to learning and attention disorders.* San Diego, CA: Elsevier Science.

Gordon, S. B., & Asher, M. J. (1994). Meeting the ADD challenge: A practical guide for teachers. Champaign, IL: Research Press.

Hinshaw, S. P., & Blachman, D. R. (2005). Attention-deficit/hyperactivity disorder in girls. In D. J. Bell, S. Foster, & E. J. Mash (Eds.), *Handbook of behavioral and emotional problems in girls* (pp. 117–147). New York: Kluwer Academic/Plenum.

Hinshaw, S., Henker, B., & Whalen, C. (1984). *Cognitive-behavioral and pharmacological interventions for hyperactive boys: Comparative and combined effects. Journal of Consulting and Clinical Psychology, 52,* 739–749.

Kaiser, N. M., & Hoza, B. (2008). Self-esteem and self-perceptions in ADHD. In K. McBurnett & L. Pfiffner (Eds.), *Attention deficit hyperactivity disorder: Concepts, controversies, new directions* (pp. 29–39). New York: Informa Healthcare.

Kapalka, G. M. (2005). Avoiding repetitions reduces ADHD children's management problems in the classroom. *Emotional and Behavioural Difficulties, 10*(4), 269–279.

Kelley, M. L. (1990). *School-home notes: Promoting children's classroom success.* New York: Guilford Press.

Kotkin, R. A. (1995). The Irvine Paraprofessional Program: Using paraprofessionals in serving students with ADHD. *Intervention in School and Clinic, 30*(4), 235–240.

Kubany E. S., Weiss L. E., & Sloggett B. B. (1971). The Good Behavior Clock: A reinforcement/time-out procedure for reducing disruptive classroom behavior. *Journal of Behavior Therapy and Experimental Psychiatry, 2,* 173–179.

Langberg, J. M., Epstein, J. N., Urbanowicz, C. M., Simon, J. O., & Graham, A. J. (2008). Efficacy of an organization skills intervention to improve the academic functioning of students with attention-deficit/hyperactivity disorder. *School Psychology Quarterly, 23*(3), 407–417.

Mikami, A. Y., Boucher, M. A., & Humphreys, K. (2005). Prevention of peer rejection through a classroom-level intervention in middle school. *Journal of Primary Prevention, 26,* 5–23.

MTA Cooperative Group. (1999). 14-month randomized clinical trial of treatment strategies for attention deficit hyperactivity disorder. *Archives of General Psychiatry, 56,* 1073–1086.

Nigg, J. T. (2006). *What causes ADHD? Understanding what goes wrong and why.* New York: Guilford Press.

Ota, K. R., & DuPaul, G. J. (2002). Task engagement and mathematics performance in children with attention-deficit hyperactivity disorder: Effects of supplemental computer instruction. *School Psychology Quarterly, 17*(3), 242–257.

Pelham, W. E., Foster E. M., & Robb J. (2007). The economic impact of attention-deficit/hyperactivity disorder in children and adolescents. *Journal of Pediatric Psychology, 32,* 711–727.

Pelham, W. E., Massetti, G. M., Wilson, T., Kipp, H., Myers, D., Newman Standley, B. B. et al. (2005). Implementation of a comprehensive schoolwide behavioral intervention: The ABC Program. *Journal of Attention Disorders, 9,* 248–260.

Pfiffner, L. J., Barkley, R. A., & DuPaul, G. J. (2006). Treatment of ADHD in school settings. In R. A. Barkley, *Attention-deficit hyperactivity disorder* (3rd ed.). (pp. 547–589). New York: Guilford Press.

Pfiffner, L. J., & McBurnett, K. (1997). Social skills training with parent generalization: Treatment effects for children with ADD/ADHD. *Journal of Consulting and Clinical Psychology, 65,* 749–757.

Pfiffner, L. J., Mikami, A. Y., Huang-Pollock, C. L., Easterlin, B., Zalecki, C., & McBurnett, K. (2007). A randomized, controlled trial of integrated home-school behavioral treatment for ADHD, predominantly inattentive type. *Journal of the American Academy of Child and Adolescent Psychiatry, 46*(8), 1041–1050.

Rapport, M. D, Murphy, A., & Bailey, J. S. (1980). The effects of a response cost treatment tactic on hyperactive children. *Journal of School Psychology, 18,* 98–111.

Taylor, B. E. S. (2007). *ADHD & me: What I learned from lighting fires at the dinner table.* Oakland, CA: New Harbinger Publications, Inc.

U. S. Department of Education, Office of Special Education and Rehabilitative Services, Office of Special Education Programs. (2004). Teaching children with attention deficit hyperactivity disorder: Instructional strategies and practices, Washington, DC. (order online: www.ed.gov/webstore/Content/search.asp).

Wang, X., Bernas, R., & Eberhard, P. (2004). Engaging ADHD students in tasks with hand gestures: A pedagogical possibility for teachers. *Educational Studies, 30*(3), 217–229.

Waschbusch, D. A., Pelham, W. E., Gnagy, E. M., Greiner, A. R., & Fabiano, G. A. (2008). Summer treatment programs for children with ADHD. In K. McBurnett & L. Pfiffner (Eds.), *Attention deficit hyperactivity disorder: A 21st century perspective* (pp. 199–209). New York: Informa Healthcare.

What Works Clearinghouse, Positive Action and Caring School Community Programs Institute of Education Sciences, U. S. Department of Education, http://ies.ed.gov/ncee/wwc.

FOR FURTHER READING:

CHADD Educators Manual on AD/HD (2nd ed.). Ziegler Dendy, C. A., Durheim, M., & Teeter-Ellison, A. (Eds.). CHADD, Washington, DC, 2006 (www.chadd.org).

Epstein, M., Atkins, M., Cullinan, D., Kutash, K., & Weaver, R. (2008). *Reducing behavior problems in the elementary school classroom: A practice guide* (NCEE #2008-012). Washington, DC: National Center for Educational Evaluation and Regional Assistance, Institute of Education Sciences, U.S. Department of Education. http://ies.ed.gov/ncee/wwc/publications/practiceguides.

Langberg, J. M. (2011). *Homework, Organization, and Planning Skills (HOPS) interventions: A treatment manual.* Bethesda, MD: National Association of School Psychologists.

McBurnett, K. & Pfiffner, L. J. (Eds.). (2008). *Attention deficit hyperactivity disorder: Concepts, controversies, new directions.* Informa Healthcare.

Rief, S. F. (2005). *How to reach and teach ADD/ADHD children: Practical techniques, strategies, and interventions* (2nd ed.). New York: Simon & Schuster.

Wolraich, M. L., & DuPaul, G. J. (2010). *ADHD diagnosis and management: A practical guide for the clinic and the classroom.* Baltimore, MD: Paul Brookes Publishing Co.

RESOURCES

Parent support groups and national organizations related to ADHD:

Children and Adults with Attention Deficit
Disorders (CHADD)
8181 Professional Place, Suite 150
Landover, MD 20785
(301) 306-7070
www.chadd.org

National Resource Center on ADHD
(800) 233-4050
www.help4adhd.org

National Attention Deficit Disorder
Association (ADDA)
PO Box 7557
Wilmington, DE 19803-9997
(800) 939-1019
www.add.org

Learning Disabilities Association of
America (LDAA)
4156 Library Road
Pittsburgh, PA 15234
(412) 341-1515
www.ldanatl.org

Association of Educational Therapists
www.aet.org

What Works Clearinghouse
Institute of Education Sciences
U. S. Department of Education
http://ies.ed.gov/ncee/wwc

National Institute of Mental Health
http://nimh.nih.gov/health/publications/
attention-deficit-hyperactivity-disorder/
complete-index.shtml

American Psychological Association
www.apa.org

Clearinghouse specializing in the sale of
books, tapes, and videos about ADHD for
parents, teachers, and children:
ADD Warehouse
300 Northwest 70th Avenue, Suite 102
Plantation, FL 33317
(800) 233-9273
http://addwarehouse.com

Web site containing downloadable
information for teachers and parents
including ratings scales, sample daily report
cards, and fact sheets:
Center for Children and Families at
University of Buffalo
http://ccf.buffalo.edu/resources_downloads.
php

INDEX

A

ADD (attention deficit disorder), 15
ADHD (attention deficit
        hyperactivity disorder)
        diagnosis of, 9, 11, 14, 17, 19, 20, 157,
                159–60, 168
        factors (causes), 6, 22–23
        girls with, 15
        outcomes, long-term, 21
        perspective, college student's, 61
        subtypes, 9–10, 12, 14–15, 154, 156, 163
        in the United States, 6

C

Child Life and Attention Skills Program,
        138, 162
Classroom Challenge, 88, 90, 97, 109, 139
classrooms
        effective, 25
        environment, 27, 28–31, 62, 141
compliance (student), 17, 65, 66, 75, 114,
        164
contracts, 89, 134, 136, 141, 143
        daily school-home, 102, 146
        homework, 122–23
        using a, 104–5
cooperative learning, 39, 40–41, 53, 54–55,
        78
curricula, 44, 62, 125
        formats, 27, 42

D

*Diagnostic and Statistical Manual for Mental
        Disorders* (DSM-IV, 1994), 9, 154,
        156

E

executive functioning, 6, 16, 18, 24

F

feedback, corrective, 25, 27, 68, 71–75, 110,
        144

G

good sport, 11, 58–59, 139
Goodsport Thermometer, 54, 56, 92

H

Home Challenge, 139
homework
        assignment planner chart, 124
        contract, 122–23
        expectations, 120–22, 144
        passes, 92–94, 126

I

ignoring (behavior), 53, 68–71
Individuals with Disabilities Education Act
        (IDEA), 5, 160

K

Kelley, Mary Lou
        School-Home Notes, 127

L

learning
        cooperative, 39–40, 54–55
        scaffold, 37, 127
lessons
        delivering, 35–38
        group, 9, 12, 35, 53, 146, 162
        interesting, 25
        involve students in, 62, 64, 140, 142
        planning, 37

M

Match Game program, 105
medication, 159, 161–64
        teacher's role in, 163
monitoring
        behaviors, 79
        peer, 40
        self, 49, 105, 107–8, 124, 141

N

neurobiological conditions, 8, 22

P

peer-to-peer
        acceptance, 41–42
        learning, cooperative, 39–41
        monitoring, 40
        problems, common, 13
        seating, 28–29
        tutoring, 39

policy, educational, 160
problems, common, 144–48
    in class, 10, 13
    at home, 12, 13
    with peers, 10, 13

R

reinforcement, positive, 23, 116, 139
    at home, 161
    praise, giving, 143
    praise, strategic, 72–74
    reinforcement, 22, 25, 49, 55, 61, 94, 95
    reinforcement center, school-based, 96
    See also token economies
report cards, daily, 96, 118, 127–35, 139
    See also token economies: Classroom Challenge
reward programs
    challenge games, 92
    classwide systems, 91–98
    fading, 95, 108
    group or team rewards, 98–102, 101, 118, 143
    privileges, 83–87, 91–96
    random, 103
    stamps (or stickers), 92
    treasure chest, 99–100
rewards
    fairness, 168
    home-based, 169
    school-based, 85
    token economies, 86 (*see also* token economies)
rewards and punishments, 24–25, 116
    response cost, 110–15, 116, 118, 131, 144, 145
    time-out, 71, 110, 116–18, 144, 147, 152–53
    work tasks, 110, 115, 117, 144 147, 152
routines, 25, 32–35, 51, 139
rules, 62–63, 72–75

S

scaffold learning, 37, 127
School-Home Notes (Kelley), 127
schoolwide programs, 94, 112, 118

self-assessment
    checklist, teacher, 141–44
    student, 48
self-esteem, 10, 12, 18, 26, 31, 39, 46, 170
self-evaluation (student), 105, 108
skills
    organizational, 39, 48, 52, 107, 139, 142
    social (training), 52–55, 61, 158, 162
    study, 48–52, 139, 160, 162
strategies
    corrective feedback, 68, 71–75, 110, 144
    educational, 25
    giving effective direction, 67
    involve students in, 64, 142
    parent and teacher, 162
    promote good attention, 27, 72, 75
    teaching, 23, 140
    test-taking, 47
    using positive attention, 68

T

teaching styles, 23, 142
technology, assistive educational, 31
Thermometer, On-Task. *See* Goodsport Thermometer
token economies, 83, 98, 143, 161
    Classroom Challenge, 88, 90, 97, 109, 139
    using, 86
treatments, 6, 7
    alternative, 164–65
    educational therapy, 162
    effective, 6, 7
    evidence-based, 161
    medication, 162 (*see also* medication)
    providing, 158
    school-based, 53
triggers (behavior), 77–79, 148

V

visual aids, 28, 30, 31, 43

W

written assignments, 44–46